BEDTIME STORIES EDITION 6

This Book Includes: "**Magic Bedtime Meditation for kids +Magic Dreams Bedtime Stories**"

By Anna Smith

Table of content

Magic Bedtime Meditation for kids

Magic Dreams Bedtime Stories

Magic Bedtime Meditation for kids

A Collection of Bed Night Stories For go to Sleep Feeling Calm and Create Their Own World of Imagination

By Anna Smith

Chapter 1:   Bedtime Adventure Stories for Kids

Nearly everybody has read a story about the adventure. In an adventure novel, someone leaves what they know, encounters risk and suspense along the way, and with a little luck, and gets safely and with a novel to share, to their final destination. Since Homer's Iliad and Odyssey there have been adventure stories around. They're rooted, in short, in human consciousness. Yet what exactly does an adventure story make? What's needed to separate a story about a trip and make it adventurous? In this class, a variety of tropes in adventure stories will be explored by exploring how such archetypes match some of the best adventure stories ever heard.

1.1. The Amazing Quest

"Burgh" grunted Owen, he was doing his homework in the house, but then he heard something odd. He glanced out to see a strange figure outside his broken glass window. He flew in the glass window which was broken. The figure had a book, a sword and a curious map of some kind. "Farewell! "Owen yelled. "Who are you?!'" "I am Merlin and I want you Owen to save The Princess Couch Potato. Here's a book about your journey, a map and a sword. "Merlin responded.

Just when Owen was going to ask how he was going to do this stuff, Merlin vanished into thin air. Owen opened the book called The Book of Ozan. Owen opened the first page to see somebody's name called Johnny Greg. He looked at the map, it had strange names and pictures of various places. There was Lake of Lettuce, Bolin's Castle, Granville Cave of Lies, Naddrins Mountain, and The Dark Lands.

"Can I just come in?" an unusual voice murmured. "Hmm, who you are? "" Owen muttered about that. The mysterious creature has not responded. Then the door opened, a tiny green owl was combined with a chipmunk and it could talk. "Hi Master Owen, Chippie is my pet." "Why are you here and how do you know my pet? "Didn't Merlin tell you that I'm your companion? "No, with this map he didn't just leave me with a sword and this book telling things about a guy named Johnny Greg." "You just told Johnny Greg? "He said in a shocked voice, 'Hm... Yeah. Is there something wrong with that?' "No, it was just Ozan's maker and guardian who escaped all the darkness and imprisoned it in another world called The Dark Land. But one day there was a mysteriously evil figure named Bolin, who hunted the good ones, including Johnny Greg. For thousands of years Bolin was the evilest. Johnny Greg speaks only to those who are the most positive and valiant of all. Owen looked out and saw a few strange things that it was a slimy yellow beast, with long razor teeth and dark pitch paws. 'Umm, what is it? "Owen asked. In surprise Chippie looked out at the fan. We will go higher! Said Chippie. "For what? "'Just run, Gloomies, they're Ozan's protectors! "Owen and Chippie sprinted from the doors of the castle and went up into a large tree. There were lots of rocks and sticks within the tree. "Should we throw rocks in the bushes over there to distract the Gloomies?" Owen asked Chippie. "Okay, but when we throw the rocks and stick, we've got to sprint out quickly, so we don't get a spot from the Gloomies." Owen and Chippie threw the rocks and sticks and sprinted away from the gates of the castle. "It was fast, yeah." "Where do we go now?" Owen asked, "I don't know, maybe check the map." Owen checked the map which had changed completely. There was a shortcut to Château Bolins! A bridge was being constructed over a ravine now, but they still had to cross Granville and the mountain of Naddrins which had a dragon on it. Owen showed Chippie and they began their once and for all trip to Dreadnars Castle.

3 Days Later………

Owen and Chippie landed at Granville, the homes were shattered everywhere and the heaps and heaps of Wicked Grannies were broken windows. "Why is this place so run down," Chippie asked Owen. "Why are there so many grannies?" Chippie responded, "I don't know why everything is missing, but I know why so many grannies are there," "Why." "Because Granville is called" The two heroes walked around the mysterious place gradually, while the Grannies were waiting.

"Why are the grannies watching us?" Owen fluttered. "I don't even remember."

The pair went on but now the Grannies approached them as if they were going to hurt them. But then a granny and a knife flew after them. "Aaaaaaaaaaaahhhhhhhhhhhhhhhhhhh!!!" Owen shouted. The Granny punched the knife at Owen. "Use your sword!" resounded Chippie. Owen took his sword and smashed it through the head of the Granny. With a great splat, the Granny's head plopped onto the ground. Blood was flying about everywhere. Just when Owen did that on Owen and Chippie all the Grannies charged. Owen slashed at the Grannies as Chippie nibbed off the Grannies limbs. They kept fighting and fighting until almost all of the grannies died. "It was rough but it felt really good as well," Owen said. "Yeah that was terrific and difficult," Chippie replied. "Where are we going then now?" Owen reviewed his chart. Owen replied: "The Bridge". But I want to get some remedies out of the potion shop first and then we should go." There were potions to sleep, potions to jump, potions to climb, potions to speed and heaps more! They got most of the potions and left Granville for walk. They marched an ally down to see a mossy cliff with vines over it. "What are we up to now?" questioned Owen. "I think I'm climbing." Chippie quickly climbed up but he obviously couldn't ascend as Owen tried. "I know how to ascend," Owen said. "I can use to scale one of the potions like the scaling potion." Owen drank an optional glug and quickly scaled the vined-covered wall.

"Wow ... Wow!! All those remedies work.

Owen looked past, a ravine with a bridge across it!

"In that diagram, this is the bridge." Owen said excitedly.

"It is Okay!"

Owen went up the bridge with Chippie the bridge wasn't what it looked like on the map. The bridge ransacked thousands of years ago. It was destroyed, planks were missing and termites all over the house. Immediately Owen tripped off the bridge and slipped. But he wasn't dead, just hurt because someone on the bridge was pulling him on, it was Chippie and another human like Merlin. "Thank you Merlin and Chippie for helping me. And why are you Merlin here? Why are you not in your village?"

Gloomies took over they assumed their chief named Scoff was murdered.

They picked Owen up and hurried away from the bridge, sprinting across the bridge.

"We are now going to the Castle of Bolin to rescue Princess Couch Potato," Owen said. "I 'm going with you now Owen," Merlin said. "You'll definitely need to beat Bolin with my magic."

The trio marched for hours and hours before they entered the castle of Bolin, which was covered by bubbling lava. They went to the gate, it was totally open, and it was like he wanted them to come. They went in cautiously and searched for any traps. They couldn't find any traps, but they walked normally. "Having come from where? "Owen asked. "I don't know but they look pretty powerful so let's hit them!!"Chippie screamed. We rushed and hacked and bashed at the soldiers, then put on their weapons. "What do I put on?"Chippie said." Drink this growing potion's glug, "Owen said. "Ok." Chippie said

Chippie drank a glug and grew to the same height as Owen. They went through the mysterious castle and saw a sign reading Bolin's Quarters-> they continued going until they reached Bolin's throne. Bolin sat on a red cushioning golden throne.

"Hello Bolin," Merlin told him. "No-see long time. Today is the day you're going to die."

The trio took the armor and Chippie fell back to normal size

"Merlin!" shrieked Bolin. "You've come here to murder me. So who are these wimps you carry with you?"

"Don't call us wimps!" both screamed.

Owen and Chippie fired their arms at Bolin.

"You'll die." Owen yelled. "Again, where is the Princess?"

"Over there." Bolin pointed to a cage she had seen with the most stunning princess Owen.

"Get her free now!!" Owen exclaimed.

"NO!!" Bolin screamed.

"Will"

The rivals fought. Owen carried his spear, Bolin carried an awful snake spear, and Merlin kept his knife in oak wood. The trio ended up pinning Bolin to the ground.

"Any last words!' shouted Owen.

"Yes." Dewsuefewruehua....

"What was it? "Owen asked puzzled

"That was a call for Naddrin to come and hear, my dragon," Bolin replied.

An evil dragon came in through the backdoor and took Bolin from him.

"You are never going to catch me!" said Bolin.

"Or, can I?" Owen said. Owen sluggled the remainder of the rising potion and grew to a giant's height.

Owen caught and knocked both Naddrin and Bolin to the ground.

To get the princess out, Owen picked up Bolin while Chippie unlocked the cage. The princess ran away, and Owen pushed Bolin in.

"What are you feeling now? Bad and in shame?" Owen asked.

Bolin did not give an answer. Owen drank the shrinking potion and shrank down to normal proportions.

1.2. A Princess

Some Years Ago, I was a young man and I used to be a friend of the Dark Lords and my name is Tim.

The Name of Dark Lords is Darth Maul .... He was a great friend but his heart turned dark and became The Dark Lord afterwards. Yeah, and if you don't already know that my name is Kingdom Fuzhou's guardian. But I wouldn't of course do it alone. By my hand is The Great Assassin ...... Tim .... he is the most powerful of all of us.

"Help us, support us with this"

"Ma'am-yes"

"He took Princess Lila from her dorm."

"We don't know who's here, but The Dark Lord is our best guess."

"We really need you. You guys think you could rescue her? It would be a long and hard Quest, but we believe that you and Tim can accomplish the task many have failed to accomplish before.

"You mean she's been taken more than once by The Dark Lord."

"Yes, that has happened a lot of times."

"You are up for the job."

"Yes, Ma'am Tim will save your daughter and me." ......

"Tim today is going to be the day that goes on the dangerous path of long life. It will take two days to rescue Princess Lila according to my calculations. Go to get your survival pack to food pouch for your armor. "Said????

"What is it with our sword?"

"Our survival pack contains the spear." WHO

"Well, let's go get our gear and go out on the journey."

...... 1 Hour later...... "James, we've got a problem "Tim began

"What are they?"

"We got back to the Demon Carnations."

"The carnations of the murderers are also Flesh-eating fish. We have 2 options that we can either pull out our swords or run I choose to pull out my sword and kill them all and thrive to the next obstacle, you are with me.

"Yes, it is my job to give you the best service I can."

"Thank you well now let Engage in Battle ......

2 Minutes on......

Tim we've defeated all of them and we can now advance to the next fearsome challenge.

"Tim," he said.

Yeah James.'

"We've come up to Quicksand."

"Well, we cannot go left because the left side is surrounded by water, and the right is surrounded by western taipans."

"But James, in the middle of the Quicksand, there are large hairy vines if we make 1 of the biggest leaps in our lives, so we can grasp the vines and pull ourselves out I'll go first. Tim said impatiently.

"Okay, I'll be right behind you, so if you catch the roots, I'll do my best to drag you down while you're as far as you can go.

.... 2 Minutes later ....

"AHHHHHHH James I fell from rugged vineyards."

"Don't worry I 'm going to go and hopefully I 'm going to do it all over, so I'm going to pull you out all right."

"The Blub."

"Well here I go these vines are so slippery now I see why Tim fell off the vine." "That hurt it was actually best that Tim landed in the Quicksand but now I have to drag him out of the Quicksand so we can keep going on the Journey to save the princess. Gee tim your big and this Quicksand is so gritty it doesn't help. You are right, Tim. "Yes, James I am but I am sticky."

"Oh, it doesn't support all of the gear being so big and dense."

"Well I'm so sad you are so poor."

"Ah, shoos, if your grip gloves did actually work, it would help."

"You should carry on dragging me out James James."

"Hey, sorry I've forgotten wow that you're great, Tim just gave way."

"Hey, as for you, I 'm good."

"No, I guess my knee was sprained"

"Alright you're right to go on"

"Indeed I believe"

"Well up next we will destroy the Forest and some people are saying Giant Possums are here.

Okay James you're about to take your sword out.

"Yeah, I seem to be fine now."

"Well let's move but be prepared because the Monster Possums can come out of the sky from the tree's ground."

"Wait for you to say they will float"

"They don't necessarily just have torn skin between the legs and the neck, so they should go that way."

"Oh yes"

"There is a possum behind you, watch out."

"Good work you kicked out, now run and take care of the first of several Demon Possums." "Everywhere on Monster Possums. Tim watch out I see light at the end of the forest run where it gets closer to the light.

Tim is here where they were. Well the Evil Grannies Lair were the evil grannies. "Yet they knew inside the evil old ladies were cooking. "We should go into the lair Tim."

"I believe we should."

"Let's go well ...."

"It's cold."

"May I impress you ah no thanks for some poison cake."

"Let me get some cake out of my way."

"No Tim its poison cake I don't eat it for the rest of our journey I need you."

"Well I'm going to leave"

"Walk quietly out the door and cross the bridge so they can catch us and make us fat with their tasty delicacies. That would have been the end of us but when we got out of there quick enough we didn't get to the end and that's good because being silent were close to the dark lords palace which means we have to be close to the Dark Lords Dragon. "They didn't know that the dragon soared 20 m over them after 5 minutes the dragon flew right in front of them and surprised them.

"Tim get out the stun gun from the dragon"

"Okay click Tim I don't think it's functioning."

"So get your weapon and Anti-Dragon Heat Shield out and I'm going to get my two out, but I'm going to get my Big Pill out as well and I'm more able to defeat the Dragon.

"Okay then I'm going to try my best to cover you just to make sure how long the Giant Pill last um is, I'm not really sure how long it's going to last but let's just hope for the best all right."
"Well I'm trying to suit and you're getting ready to cover me up. Okay on 3 we 're running and standing away from me because when I grow the dragon is going to blow fire straight at me and he's going to be so focused on me that you can gradually climb his back and take the dragon collar thingy then hopefully it's going to fly so we can keep going. Okay on three 1, 2, 3 go Tim, how do you get down there?

"Good but be alert!! The dragon is looking at you James

"Thanks but Tim start climbing back to the dragons"

"Good.....James I'm near that collar thingy

"This part of the dragon is very vulnerable, we'll be really careful so climb very, very slow"

"James I've got to a shirt"

"Okay, it would have a loop at the back of his face."

"I find that I'm going to open it then I'm going to launch so you can grab me all right."

"Okay. Arrrrrgggggghhhhhh James pick me up"

"I do have you"

"Tim fell off the dragon while you were falling just as we guessed"

"Yes that stupid Dragon is gone"

"Okay Tim lets hide around the castle's back, so we won't be seen creeping around the castle's edge"

"Yeah I 'm happy with that"

"Great and quiet stroll ....

4 minutes ago....

Hey Tim look at those garden gnomes they're not a little strange for an evil nest

"Wow, for a bad lair, they're really strange .... James the flying Garden Gnomes

"Why not dumb Garden Gnomes are not going! Tim one does have me

"James didn't make us bottle you"

"Okay yes"

"But that doesn't mean we can break them if we find any bricks"

"Yeah it does but maybe it's too loud"

"Yeah, maybe it's just too loud to find some rocks while you fight off some of the other gnomes so you can help me get more rocks."

"Okay, I can handle that." "Tom, I'm happy to help but we can want to do it faster"

"Okay" When Tim and James went on discovering more rocks they didn't realize that there were a lot of booby traps inside on the way to the very top of the castle that was Princess Lila.

"Tim I think we've got enough rocks to smash them all OK on 3 we run and smash them all 1, 2, 3 go Arrrrrrrrrrrrrrrrrrrrrrrrrrrrrr"

"Tim I believe we all got them"

"Good then let's go to the palace"

1.3. A wizard

My name is Corrin, my nation's warrior / hero (who has a mild fear of eggs!). I was hanging out in my castle penthouse when

Sizzly the Wizard burst out and called out "Ragnarok used the Dread Charm! Eventually, it will enter us and cause all life to wane! "Dread the scorn? Ragnarok, or not? Wait, and what!? "And I said. There were so many doubts running through my mind. "Wasn't Ragnarok the Unholy exiled to Skull Island because his dark thoughts were rising beyond the reach of the King? "I was wondering. "Weeeeeeelllll, kind of a sort of, maybe the spell wasn't strong enough." To do it. In the end! "I was shaking.

I leapt out the window and over the roof of the house of my companion Bumblebear. "It's time for fun!!"And I screamed. I jumped on his back and we ran running. I heard Sizzly shouting from behind "poor yeah, more damage to property? Hyah!" To the Castle of the Queen! "I was asking Bumblebear. When I did a double backflip off of him we got to the tower's foot and landed with a thump. Once I saw the vacant seat I strolled in casually and discovered she was gone. "I told Sizzly to let you know she's gone." said the king. "Oh, I still quit to learn the details, too early. I shall be with your father again! "When I raced down the hall to Bumblebear, I shouted back to the king and queen.

We went into town to challenge certain people who have a history of dealing with Ragnarok but many of the villagers are decent people who keep away from such dark wizards as he. The first person we interrogated was Malcumus, a local blacksmith. "Where were you today, at 21:00? "So I told him. He responded,

"Just finishing off on new Electranium sword and shield sets to pick up today's elite armies. Why? For what? "This is classified information. Thank you! "I wrote, and we're gone.

"There just isn't anyone else to ask," I told Bumblebear. He groaned in pain. "Not worried! "I sent him assurances. "We are going to find Princess Lucina! Everything we do is! "Wait!!! Wait! "We are hearing a voice. Malcumus runs towards us. "I forgot to give you your own sword and shield on Electranium," he said. "It can harness the power of electricity and turn into a ball of pure energy without end. I'll give you another stinger so Bumblebear can absorb it and shoot it." "Thanks! "I said, and we headed to inspect the system of defense.

Something must have gone off about this, because Ragnarok should never have sneaked by it. She was absolutely blind. I saw some sort of mystical texture playing around broken machine parts. Everywhere, there were cogs and stone bricks and any mound of rubble had its magic look. "These lives must avenge themselves," I told Bumblebear. He was raging with rage and remorse.

Our last stop before we left our Electranium boat was the statue of Goddess. Most guerrillas went to the statue of Goddess to pray for support. We got to the statue and I prayed for my future. Even if you ask why our nation has so much Electranium in Gokusaiyan, I'll tell you. Thousands and thousands of years ago, while an electrified meteor crashed into a deserted island during Chaetophere's Great War. The meteorite's influence evolved into the Ever tree, a legendary tree capable of developing pure branched electranium. Small mushroom warriors protect the tree with arrows and poisonous fungus bombs but we have made friends with them and we can take as much Electranium as we need for our protection needs and weaponry. They had naming rights, because they were the first life to walk among it. It was called Nidavellir, by its inhabitants.

We make our way to the harbour. The harbor is just behind the forts. Some of the vessels are attached to the royal family's ships or land. I am of course part of the fleet so I have my own boat. Bumblebear is big enough to lay down, so I climb on top of him. He is quite relaxed and gentle too. We are sailing down to Nidavellir to see what's going on. We're ambushed, as soon as we get there. I realize Ragnarok's brainwashed mushroom guys. They seem to be really nice. "Seems like a series of battles is coming up! And I told Bumblebear.

He was growling with anticipation. Beat Down! CLANG On! BOOM BOOM! CLATTER Down! SMASH On! PICKNOW! We pounded on their tiny little poison heads for an explanation! They have even a poisonous spore on their heads in their round thingies. They start waking up and scratching out their spores. "Shhhhrrrrrriiiiieeeeeeekkkkk" shrieked in pain. "Everyone is sorry! They've been brainwashed! "Yeeeeeeeeeeeeeee!"It is the merged Mushroom Individual Species' official language.

Mushroom Soup is a forbidden meal on our island too. We have a connection with them too soon.

Each of them had a little piece of metal cut out. "It's an Aetherstone." he said. Upon it came a warning. It was Ragnarok's. He told me that he had a fun surprise concerning his aunt, the wicked queen Bayonetta. I wasn't persuaded yet.

They gave me the Aetherstone and some arrows for the electric bomb. I switch it on and see what they're doing. Suddenly a red fluid erupted from it, and it formed into a disk. Within, the mushrooms tell me that this is part of the Aether.

I thank them for their assistance and I'm going back to my ships. We head off towards the misty, dark abyss which the light seems to inhale. Giant spinning hands stand over the gateway to the vortex. The vortex points to the wicked super castle wizard / witch Ragnarok, who has lots of warlords and warlocks fighting with him around it. Suddenly a blue-jacketed skeleton dropped out of a tree onto the ships. "Hey guys!!!!! "The skeleton said. It said something about how much it despises Ragnarok and Bayonetta and was expendable something about which he was proud of his army and wanted to help me seal the darkness and stop it.

"What's your name" I finally asked it. "Sans, but why are you asking?" "Because you are now an official member of the Apex Primitives!" I said to it. "Also, do you have an official gender?" "Of course! I'm a male, obviously!" "Yeah, thought so!"

We were sailing towards the inky abyss. Unexpectedly an army of mega hands surround us. "We're under attack!!!!" I yelled. Some dark lightning came crashing down and obliterated the hands. "Huh, how convenient!" said Sans. "But still, I could have done it myself! I have power over time and space!"

We opened and inhaled a dark, yellow passage. There was all confusion and rubble around us. I shuddered at the thought that I was moving here again. "LOOOOOOOOOOOOUUUUUUUTTTTTT!! "Sans cried. It was Rixium, Dream World king and one of the old Villain Bar mates from Ragnarok. A Dreamy Dust storm exploded into the air. Bumblebear screamed the Old Roar and shot the Dreamy Dust at Rixium straight away. He'd snoring flat in no time. "I didn't think even Dreamy Dust will work on Rixium," I said. "The universe at least is working to our favor, this time around! "And Sans said.

He pulled a grappling hook out and tornado spun us up to the castle's highest spire but we all fell off and went way up and into Ragnarok 's room into his pool of sheets and blankets in which he sleeps. "OOOOOOOOOOOOOOOOOOOOOOFFFFFFFFF!!!!!!

"We've said that. "Why does the world currently work so well in our favor?!? "Sans said.

TTTHHHUUMMMMPPPPP!!!! (Capitalized because it is loud) "WAAAAAAAAAAHHHHHH!!! "Sans shouted. PPPPEEEEEWWWWWW PPPPPPEEEEEEEEWWWWW went to a mystery number on my electronic bomb arrows. WAS IT A DUMMY!!! They saw a light and a kazipp and Ragnarok and his partner came in so they were condensed into a demo-bokoblin. "See which one is here! "And I said. In return, I got a Growl. This demo-form appears to have induced Ragnarok to lack his intellect. "Never mind! I will have you with me at any moment! "I yelled, and swung my spear.

RRRROOOOOAAAAAARRRRRRRRRR!!!! Let's move on!!! Bumblebear flew to his head, shooting electrical energy from his stinger, and I shot arrow after arrow after arrow after arrow after arrow, but part of his hide was too thick to peer out. I found his tail a bit glowing. A-HA!! A poor point! Though I don't like them, I tossed a few eggs at his butt.

AAAAARRRRRRGGGGGGGHHHHHHHHHHHH!!!!! It poofed back into Ragnarok so we had the Lady of Destruction's planet out of us. Now we ought to be concerned with the Dark World God. NOOOOOOOOOO! "He screamed. "YYOU!! "And he wrote, referring to Sans. "FIGHT ME TO FORTH The WORD!! "Nah, I'm all right! "Sans said. "I would have liked a dance-off!

Try to try to get the most out of me? "" "NOOOO!! LOCK AWAY ME!! NEVER, I WANT TO DANCE!! Ragnarok yelled.

"We did have something better for you actually! POCUS Au HOCUS!!! "And I said. Now He's been exiled. During the banishment the princess mystically came back. "Hello everyone! Let's just go home! "Princess Lucina said. There was a light and a burst of chiming and we were standing at the foot of the tower of queen. "Wait." .. Wait! Couldn't you do that to get us over there?!? "And I told. "My magic powers were diminished by the tower and I couldn't mind flying to my destination," the princess said.

"Ah well, well! We were having a fun time, at least! "Everybody smiled and cheered that the princess was free once more. And for years no other attack came upon Gokusaiyan. 26 Until 31 December ...

1.4. The Pirate Ship

Once upon a time there was a little boy named Harry whose vision was to get his own pirate ship and sail across the seas; to discover gold that had long, long ago been lost.

Harry also spent his weekends with his grandmother and grandfather; his mother would drop him off at 9 o'clock on the dot every Saturday morning and pick him up at 6 o'clock only after tea time on Sundays.

Grandma and Granddad's home was a huge old farmhouse with a big greenhouse and next to a grassy field full of lovely flowers. Granddad's workshop and an ancient shed were at the edge of the yard.

One sunny Sunday morning Harry sat with his Granddad breakfast at the table and told him he had a dream the night before he was captain of a pirate ship searching for treasure chest. Granddad told little Harry "well you need a treasure map to locate some lost treasure Pirates! And little Harry and his grandparents spent all the sunny afternoon designing a map to trace the hidden treasure. There were other risks for Pirates looking for treasure and by the time they had done the map revealed sharks and puddles and would have to conquer many little Harry Pirates.

Harry's mother came to drive him home and he gave him a kiss farewell to his granddad, and he always worried of the pirate ship and the stolen treasure.

The next day Harry's Granddad wanted to start designing Harry's pirate ship from his imagination to impress him with the weekend that followed. It'd take him a long time if Granddad got to work early! Granddad knew he wanted plenty of wood to create a magnificent pirate ship and looked into the garden where he saw his old shed that had been stood there for years, "that's it," Granddad said to himself, "I can use the wood from the old shed."

Granddad opened the shed door to discover an old car steering wheel from a car he had several years before and also an old bell which used to hang on the shed door, grandfather thought they were going to use it for the pirate ship, so he put them to one side and began tearing down the old shed. He put all the wood planks out on the garden and after all the shed had been torn down, he took all the wood planks into his workshop where he could cut the wood and start building the dream pirate ship for little Harry.

Grandpaa worked on building the pirate ship for the next few days getting up early each morning and only stopping when Grandma would call out loudly in the garden "your delicious tea is hot and ready!"

Friday soon came around, and Friday was market day in the town, Grandma always went to the market on a Friday to do her shopping. Before setting off Grandma asked Grandfather "is there anything you need?"

"Yes," grand ather replied, "there's a flag-selling stall on the market, could you please wait for the big pirate flag to be placed on top of Harry's pirate ship? "

Off grandmother went with her grocery bag and a list of all the items she wanted to sell.

Grandfather soon had time to paint the pirate ship and fit the old steering wheel he had discovered in the shed. Grandfather fastened the wheel towards the front of the pirate ship and the ancient bell to the back; "I thought the bell would come in very handy and offer little Harry something to ring if he put his fantasy pirate ship in danger" Grandfather discovered some old rope and some old bedding at the back of his workshop which he would use to create a sail for the ship, all he required now was for Grandmother to return with the pirate flag so he could place it at the top of cute Harry's pirate ship

Saturday morning was the day of the amazing surprise for little Harry and at 9 o'clock on the dot he arrived running down the path with a big cute smile on his face. The first thing Harry said: Hi Grandma, where is my Grandfather?!" "He's down in the garden" Grandma replied "but before you set off, don't I get a hug?"

"Oh sorry Grandmother," said Harry and he gave his Grandmother a big hug and off he ran to find his Grandfather.

Granddad dragged the pirate ship out of the warehouse and into the meadow, so that Harry could continue playing as his ship's captain. Little Harry climbed into the ship and started to steer the way and loop the globe to warn the other Pirates that he now had his ship and was about to discover the treasure

"Do you forget something? "Grandad inquired about the treasure map they had made the week before, when he walked by Harry.

Grandfather was back at the cottage, making a cup of tea. He was seated at the table reading his newspaper feeling very delighted that he had made the fantasy pirate ship Harry had.

Harry was on his ship giving orders to his crew when unexpectedly the grass in the meadow turned from green to a deep sea blue and his ship started bobbing up and down on the waves "wow" thought Harry "it is a magic pirate ship! Now I can really go and discover the hidden treasure!"

Harry eventually reached the island, after hours and miles of sailing. This was much smaller than when he first saw it out at sea on his pirate ship, it was only around the size of Granddad's back yard. "Never mind," he said, "the smaller the safer, because the missing treasure will be harder to search."

Harry climbed tightly from his ship to his map. The path he and his grandfather drew the week before showing him which way to go and when he reached a small tree, he began digging. With no luck he dug a hole, so he tried a little further along the path again. Harry was digging around when he discovered something heavy all of a sudden, it was a small wooden shell. He removed away the sand and pulled the top open. There were tons of glittering gold coins inside the package "Sure! I find the gold "yelled Harry.

He picked up the box and turned to head back down the path to his pirate ship. Little Harry soon got to know that he had forgotten to fasten the ship to anything when he first arrived at the island and he had been so busy digging he hadn't noticed that his pirate ship had sailed away.

"Oh no!" thought Harry, "How am I going to get back home to Grandfather   and   Grandmother?!" Harry sat down and began to weep. All of a sudden little Harry heard a voice, Grandfather's voice, shouting his name. Harry asked "How did you find me?"

"You slept on your pirate ship" grandfather replied "you must have dreamed"

Little Harry got up and managed to climb out of his pirate ship and began on his magical pirate ship telling his granddad all about his dream. "And what is that in Harry's pocket? "grandfather asked, and he found a shiny gold coin when Harry checked.

This story is dedicated to those little boys and all the little girls who have a dream, but some are magical.

Always keep your dream going.

Chapter 2: Bed-Time fables for kids to Sleep

2.1 The Trawler & Monkey

A Monkey sitting on such a high oak saw many Fisherman tossing the traps into a stream, watching the acts closely. After a bit, the fisher decided to give up hunting then leaving the traps on the bank as they went home for dinner. The Rodent, the most impressionistic of creatures, came down from base of the peak and attempted to do what they had intended. He had managed the net, and dropped everything into the water, but got caught up in the fibers. While sinking, he said it to himself, "I got caught justifiably; with what purpose did I have to go to eat the fish that I never saw a mesh?"

2.2 The Fish & the Fisherman

One day, a Fisher who worked on his mesh' produce got one little fish as a result of the labor of his day. The salmon, gasping twitching, begged for his living: "How nice could I be to oneself, gentlemen, just how small am I valuable? I haven't reached full scale yet. Praise god to save my soul, and carry me back into the water. I will quickly become such a huge fish, prepared for the wealthy's desks; and perhaps you'll capture me anew, so make an amazing profit from me. "The fisher responded," I really would be a quite simpler man, unless, just for sake of larger uncertainty, I would forsake my present benefit.

2.3 The Lion & Doe

A DOE pushed hard by predators reached a refuge cell that owned to a Lion. As once Lion saw her coming, then covered herself; however as she was hidden in the pit, he leapt over her and ripped her to strips. "Pity seems to be me," bellowed the Doe, "that fled from person, just to toss myself into the ferocious predator's belly! "This must be considered to prevent one wicked consideration not to slip into the next.

2.4 The Brant And The Swan

A wealthy individual from bought a Goose as well as a Swan at the auction. He had fed one just for his bowl, and managed to keep others for his music's sake. So when opportunity arose to slaughter the brant, the chef decided to take him at sunset, while it was pitch black, and he could not differentiate between one bird while the other, and captured the Whooper instead of the Brant. Physically attacked, the Swan broke out into music, making oneself recognized by his tone, or by his melodies saving his live.

A phrase is much more valuable in period.

2.5 The Craftsman His Boy & the Donkey

A MILLER with his child rode their donkey to a market next door to auction him. They hadn't traveled that far before they found a female's unit gathering around a pool, chatting and laughing. "Glance after that," one amongst them started to cry, "If you've ever seen these chaps wandering upon this pavement since they could start riding? "The one. Having heard that, the elderly man easily mounted his boy on the Donkey, then rode joyously along through his side. Currently they have come up in serious conversation with a party of elderly folks. "Hey," one of them have said, "this reveals whatever I intended. In such times what value is given to an elderly? Can you see the lazy boy ride whilst walking alongside his elderly dad? Get down, hello youthful scapegrace, then let the elderly fella relax his tired legs. * * After all that elderly man dismounted his child, and he got back up. They still hadn't gone this far in the direction just before they reached a women's and children's club: "how some, you fat elderly gentleman," screamed a few dialects simultaneously, "why would you travel on the behemoth, although this destitute tiny gent would hardly be able to cope pace with you? Apart from him, the well-natured Crafts-man ended up taking up his boy. They'd almost entered the city. "Praise god, decent man," a resident said, "is it your own Donkey? Yeah," the elderly man replies. "Well, I wouldn't have gone that way," the latter stated, "after mounting him. How some, you 2 chaps are smarter capable of carrying the poor animal than what you are." "Anything and everything to satisfy you, "the elderly man stated;" we know there won't but attempt. "So, lit up with his boy, they fastened the donkey's limbs together and managed to carry him on their forearms across an overpass close to the city's entrance with support of a lamp post. This amusing image managed to bring the throngs of people to giggle at this; until the donkey did not like the commotion, nor even the bizarre carrying to which he had been subjected, ended up breaking the straps which bonded him, & fell into the water, sliding off the lamp post. The elderly man, incensed & embarrassed, tried to make the best of his return trip anew, persuaded that he's never satisfied anyone by wanting to satisfy, and losing his donkey in the process.

2.6 A Chandelier

A Chandelier poured in so much lubricant, or too much arcing, proclaimed it provided greater illumination than sky. It was quickly extinct, by just one rapid burp of air emerging. Its holder lit it up and was like: "don't really boasting that much, but be happy to quietly offer the flame. Learn that the star don't always need a relight

2.7 The two Toads

Two Toads took up residency in the same lake. Beneath the hot weather, the reservoir was gone dry, they decided to leave it and cast out for the next residence next to each other. Since they walked together across they happened to come to pass a big well, adequately filled of water, viewing which of the toads stated to another, "Let's go down and make our stay in this well: it will provide us with basic necessities." the latter responded of greater caution, "But if the water should fail us, how can we get out of such a profusion anew?

"Never do anything without remembering the implications.

2.8 The Vain Fox

Witnessing significant flour and beef dumped by herders in the hole of a pine, a Fox, extremely famished, crept into in the pit, and managed to make a delicious lunch. Just before he managed to finish, he was really packed that he couldn't even come out, but very unfortunately started to shriek and bemoan. Another Fox passed along, noticed his wails and managed to come up and questioned about the motive of his complaint. He replied to him since he learned what has just actually occurred, "ohhh, you're hoping to stay here anyway, my buddy, once you become like you had been when you crawled in, and you're going to get through conveniently."

2.9 The Woodman & the Tracker

A Tracker, not really brave, was looking for a Lion's footprints. He inquired a person in the woods who was dropping elms if he'd seen the signs of his footprints, or if he did know where his cave would have been. "I 'm going to," he stated, "reveal you the Lion himself in one go," answered the trapper, becoming quite gaunt, conversing his dentures out of dread, "sorry, thank you. I did not even ask that; it was only I'm in quest of his route, not really the Lion itself. "The champion is incredibly brave in actions and speech.

2.10 The Bull & the Rat

A Mouse stung a Bull, and wanted to catch him, sickened by that of the bite. The Mouse initially entered "his cavity in protection, as well as the Bull digged into the walls of his paws, until after maddened, lying prone back, he napped by the pit. The Mouse poking out, creeping shiftily up his back, and yet again trying to bite him, returning to his pit. The Bull arising, but not realizing how to go about it, became regrettably flummoxed.

2.11 The Cock & the Thieves

few robbers went to a house, & discovered nothing except a cock, which they managed to steal, and went off quite quickly as they should have; however when they returned home, they planned to kill the cock, that begged however for his life: please, save me; I am very beneficial to people, and I cheer them up to their job in the twilight. That's also exactly why we should kill you, "they responded;" because when you start waking up your neighbors, you bring disaster to our business.

Virtuous protections are full of hate to the disposed wickedness.

2.12 The Dog & the Chef

A Wealthy man had a wonderful meal, and decided to invite numerous colleagues and friends to it. His beagle took the opportunity to host a peculiar dog, a buddy of him, stating, "My owner offers a festival; you will also have exceedingly good praise; end up coming and dine with me later this evening." The beagle so invited arrived at the scheduled time, and seeing the arrangements for such a great event, replied, "Very happy I am that I have come! I don't really have a moment like this. I'm supposed to take care as well as eat enough just to last me both tonight and tomorrow. "While he was thus congratulating himself & wagging his tail, as if to establish a sense of his enjoyment to his buddy, the chef saw it to shifting by many his meals, and, capturing him by his forehead and leg paws, packaged him out of the door without celebration. He dropped to the ground with intensity, then ran back off, hurling badly. His shouting quickly prompted other stray dogs who went towards him and asked whether he had He ate his meal. He responded, "How some, I did drink so much whisky to say you the reality, that I do not memorize anything. I don't realize when I came out from the building. "Uninvited visitors never collide a welcoming.

2.13 The Dancing Chimp

An Heir to the throne had taught other chimps to dance. Being obviously perfect imitators of the acts of people, they proved them to be among the most suitable students; & they danced as much as any of the princes when lined up in the wealthy clothing and costumes. The show was always replicated with great applause, before a prince, intent on mayhem on one occasion, took a couple of peanuts out of his jacket and hurled them onto the floor. Just at appearance of the peanuts, the chimps lost their dance and were (since they were even so) animals rather than performers, taking off their costumes and ripping their garments, struggling over the nuts with each other. Thus the dance show ended, despite the audience's amusement and scorn.

2.14 The Fox & the Farmer

A Farm worker, involves a strong bitterness with a Fox for looting his chicken field, eventually caught it &, compelled to take enough vengeance, bound some tether to his tail quite saturated in oil, & set fire. The Fox fled to the rancher's farm by a mysterious fatal accident that had captured him. This was the period of the harvest season; but that year, the farm worker did not harvest anything, and came back home sorely mourning.

2.15 The Luck & the Traveler

A Traveler, maddened with a difficult trip, lied at the edge of a shallow well surmounted by exhaustion. Within one inch of slipping and falling in well, Lady luck it is said, popped up to him, shacking out of his sleep, and so addressing him: "good fellow, awake, for if you would have gone down into the water, the fault will be laid on me, and I'll have a bad reputation among demigods; for I discover that guys will surely attribute their catastrophes to me, even so well that they have decided to bring of them with their own foolishness.

Each is more or less master of his own destiny.

2.16 The kittiwake & the Kite

A Kittiwake bolted too big a fish, rupture its depth gullet-bag and laying down to demise on the coast. A kite who saw him bellowed: "You owe your destiny lushly; for there is no market for a bird of air to pursue their fresh produce from of the ocean."

A man should be happy to call his own affairs.

2.17 The Bald Warrior

Warrior wore a wig and flew out hunting. His cape & wig shook by a sudden burp of air, where a boisterous giggle popped from his crew mates. He pulled his stallion, and ended up joining in the pun with great pleasure, trying to say, "how many wonderment that strands of hair which aren't really mine must float away from me, once they have betrayed even the guy who built them: with someone they were also bom! ”

2.18 The Oaks & the Jupiter

THE oak trees lodged a petition with Jupiter, stating, "We take on the burden of nature in no way, because of all the woods that rise we are by far the most constantly in danger of the axes." Jupiter replied, "You just have to praise yourself for the failings where you're subjected: for if you've not rendered these outstanding columns and supports, and prove yourself so beneficial to the roofers and the ranchers the axes might not constantly be used to your stems.

2.19 The Fox Lion and the Donkey

The fox the lion, and the donkey agreed to help one another in the hunt. 3After securing a huge tush, the Lion kept asking the donkey, on such their come back from woods, to allocate their proper fraction to each of the 3 partners in the agreement. The donkey divided the ruin cautiously into 3 parallel shareholdings, and respectably suggested that the other two make the first selection. The Lion swallowed the Donkey, breaking out a massive anger. After which he asked the Fox to consider making him a segment The Fox gathered everything they had eaten into one big stack, and left the tiniest crumb to himself. The Lion replied, "Who educated you the craft of split, my quite amazing associate? You're good for a fragment. "Fox responded," By observing donkey's destiny.

Happy is the guy who knows from other people's misfortunes.

2.20 The Cabinet maker & the image of Mercury

A really poor fella, a cabinet maker through trade, had such a timber portrait of Mercury, upon which he continually made prayers, and begged the idol to make him money: but he became beggars despite his delights. Finally, becoming quite furious, he brought his photo down from his plinth & smashed that against the wall: when his head was pushed off, a flow of gold poured out, easily identified by the craftsman, and then said, "after all, I believe you're very inconsistent and unjustified; for when I compensated you honor, I didn't get any benefits: but now that I'm mistreating you, I'm filled with an excess of money."

2.21 The Cheetah & the Fox

THE FOX and thus the cheetah were disputing who of the two was the most stunning. One after the other the cheetah showed the various areas that adorned his coat. The Duck, disrupting him, replied, "To see how much more lovely I 'm extremely, that is adorned, not really in body, but in spirit."

2.22 The Rabbit & the Lion

A Lion happened to come along a Rabbit, sleeping fast on her form. He was only in the process of capturing her, as a wonderful young Hart churned past, leaving the Hare to pursue. The Hare awakened, startled by the sound, and scuddled backwards. After a foot hunt the Lion was unable to catch the Hart and came back to eat on the Hare. After realizing that the Rabbit went far away, he stated, "I'm done rightly, for having let go of the food I had in my hand for the chance to get more."

2.23 A Scholar Mercury & the Ant

A Scholar observed the wreckage of a ship from the coast, some of which perished the passengers and crew. He railed against the unfairness of Syracuse, who could permit far too many helpless individuals to die horribly just for one unlawful mayhap boating in the vessel. Has he indulged in those thoughts, he realized himself circled by an entire force of Ants, He was standing near their nest. One of ant crawled up and bitten him, but with his feet he promptly stomped upon them all to destruction. Mercury came in and striking the Scholar with his wand stated, "Tell me how come you became a judge of the Syracuse, who hast thyself in a similar manner behaved with helpless Ants?"

2.24 An Eagle & the Farmer

A Farmer spotted an Eagle trapped in a net, and cut him loose, much appreciating the eagle. The Eagle did not indicate unsympathetic to his bearer for finding him sitting underneath a wall that was not secure, he flew for him, snatching a package settling on his head with his legs and letting the package fall again upon his rising to chase him. The farmer picked it up and returned to the same position and saw the wall from which had fallen on the floor; and he was deeply surprised just at Eagle's appreciation for the support he had given him.

2.25 The Craftsman and the Jupiter

A Craftsman, chopping down timber by a river basin edge, let his axe sink into a plunge river by disaster. Having thus been stripped of the source of his survival, he sat on the edge of river, lamenting his harsh destiny. Jupiter appeared, & sought his tears triggered, he informed him his tragedy Jupiter, lifting a gold axe, questioned if it was the one he had missed. On his claiming that it wasn't his, Mercury vanished a second term under the water and emerged with a silver axis in his pocket, once asking "if it was his" of the Workman. Upon the Workman claiming it wasn't, he dived into the water for the third time and pulled up the missing axis. Jupiter, delighted with his loyalty, offered him the golden & silver axes other than his own, on the craftsman requesting it, and voicing his delight at his restoration.

After arriving back home the craftsman told everything that had happened to all his friends and fellows. One of them settled just to try to see if he'd not secure himself the same great luck as well. He raced to the river and intentionally flung his axis into the water at the same spot, and sat to sob on the shore.

Jupiter appears to him only as he wished he might; and when he had discovered the source of his sorrow, he plummeted into the sea, lifted a golden ax, and asked about it, he had fallen. The worker grudgingly grabbed it, and proclaimed it was the very same axis he had missed from a reality. Jupiter, disappointed at his venality, not only threw the gold axes away, but declined to retrieve for him the axis he had tossed into the sea.

2.26 Two Troopers & the Robber

A robber came across2 troopers riding alongside. The one escaped down the road; second stepped on his floor, although with his pilsner dominant wrist attempted to defend oneself. The Robber becoming vanquished, the timid partner comes running and pulls his blade, but instead, tossing back his traveling robe, says, "I 'm going to him, and I'm going to take care he's going to discover where he's hit." He who battled with the Perpetrator said, "I really believe yon had supported me right now, even if it was just with those letters, because I would have been motivated to believe them. Even so, I, who've expexed at what pace you're running from, know well that you can't put any reliance on your bravery.

2.27 The Mercury Elephant & the Lion

The Lion's constant grievances grown weary the Jupiter. "It's accurate," he replied, "O Mercury! Which I am enormous in toughness, Lovely in element, and mighty in assault. I have dentures in my fangs, and fangs in my feet, and I reign it over some beasts. Wilderness; and how disgraceful it is since I am, I ought to be afraid of A cock carping. "Mercury responded," why would you keep blaming me without a cock carping offered you all the qualities I possessed Acquire me and you'll never fail your bravery for only this instance at this the Lion He grumbled, and regretted deeply, reproaching oneself for his cowardliness, and desiring that he could die. As these feelings carried via his imagination, he encountered an Elephant, and got close to talk to him. He noticed, after a while, that the Elephant very often raised his ears, and he asked what the issue was, or why his ears relocated with a temblor every now and again. Just then a Gnat resolved on the Elephant's body, and he answered, "Are you seeing that little bubbling insect? If it gets into my head, then my fate is sealed. Now I'm meant to die. "The Lion stated," Well, because such a big beast is scared of a tiny gnat, I'm not going to whine anymore, I'm not going to want to be gone. Even if I am,

I consider myself better off than the Lion, to the point that a Cock is superior to a Gnat.

2.28 The Kite & the Eagle

AN Eagle, filled with grief, settled in contact with a kite on the limbs of a tree. "Why," stated the Kite, "with quite ruinous appearance do I perceive you?" I 'm looking for a compatible partner for me," she responded, "and I didn't locate one." "Consider taking me," said the kite; "I'm much bigger than you are." "Why are you able to obtain the way of making a living with your pillage? "OH, I always captured and kept an ostrich in my paws. "Convinced by such phrases, the Eagle welcomed him as her friend. Soon after the wedding ceremony, the Eagle said, "travel apart, and cheer me up the ostrich that you pledged me." The Kite, rocketing up in the air into the air, revived the dirtiest mouse probable, and stinked about it for a long time. Oh. "Is this a truthful fulfilling of the pledge to me?" the Eagle asked. "The Kite answered," There is nothing I wouldn't have vowed in order to meet your imperial face, whatever else I knew I had to disappoint in the results.

2.29 The Painted Lion & the Monarch's Boy

A Monarch who only had 1 son, loving of military activities, had a vision to alarm him that a lion might kill his child. Scared the Dream was to be real, he designed a nice mansion for his son and decorated his halls with all manner of wildlife of the scale of life, including a lion's image. Whenever the future king see it, his sorrow at being so constrained exploded out again, and, remaining by the lion, he shouted like this: Oh the very repugnant of animal species? By my father's false nightmare, that he saw in his bed, in this pace I am encaged because of you, as if Was a lady; what am I going to do something to you?" with all these expressions he extended forth his arms towards that bramble-tree, intending to break off a piece from his roots so that he could fight the beast, until one of his sharp prickles stabbed his palm, causing considerable swelling and pain, such that the future king collapsed into a weak fall. A high fever through which he expired not that many days later unexpectedly setting in.

We had best bravely put up without problems than trying to stop them.

2.30 The Country man and the Oaf

A Wealthy nobles once un-chargedly decided to open the theaters to the citizens, and tried to give public announcement that he'd be nicely rewarding anyone to devise a new enjoyment for the particular evening. The award was contested by numerous public artists. Among them came a common oaf with his humor, claiming he had something of an entertaining that had not even been put out on any level. The spreading of this report created a fantastic splash in the location, but in every portion the theater was congested. The oaf popped up on the platforms on its own, with no apparatuses or secessionists, and the very perception of assumption triggered a strenuous quietness. Unexpectedly the oaf lowered his face to his chest He mimicked with his tone the screeching of a little pig so excellently that the crowd proclaimed that even under his robe he would have a heffer he requested that it be shook out. They applauded the performer when it was concluded and but nothing is being discovered, and packed him with loudest ovations. A crowded compatriot, seeing all that had happened, muttered, "Save me, merlin, at that move he can't match me! "And immediately asserted that the next day he would be doing the similar stuff, albeit in a far more conventional manner. A larger turnout gathered in the theater on the morning; but now partiality persisted quite largely for their favorite actor, and the viewer's went to deride the Countryman rather than seeing the freak show.

Even then, all actors emerged on the floor. The oaf first sighed and snuck away after getting the standing ovation and claps from the onlookers, as on the previous day. Then, the Countryman started, trying to hide a very little pig under his garments (that he did actually, but not expected of the viewer),produced to lay hold of it and tug his ear as he started to wheeze, and convey in his distress the pigs 's true scream. The audience, even so, with one assent cried out that the oaf had provided a much more accurate impersonation, and began to cry out to pull the Countryman out of theater. The rustic generated little pig out of his robe on this, and demonstrated the goodness of their error by the most optimistic facts. "Look here," he said, "this reveals the kind of jurors that you are."

2.31 Water In The Desert

Once, a boy was raised in a family called Bodhisatva, baptized Vaishya. The family has had a thriving business. When Bodhisatva grew older, he began to assist in the family company. Often he had to travel to other cities to search for water in the desert for company. When Bodhisatva and some five hundred entrepreneurs went on a business tour, we all had their carts of the bullock. The leader cart was leading upfront, and others followed him. The caravan came gradually to the mountains. None to be seen everywhere but sandy desert. After traveling such a long distance through the desert, they all felt exhausted. It was impossible to go on since the sun was too bright.

Seeing all of this, the caravan leader said, "Let's stop here for the day. We'll start our trip in the evening, and then the conditions will be pretty good." They parked their carts in bullock, gave the bulls fodder and water, and went to rest. The caravan leader yelled out in the evening, "O guys get ready for the ride. They're not that far out. We're going to get there in the morning."

Everyone got ready, and one after the other Bullock carts made a long queue. Weight reduction on the bullock carts. They drained the vessel of water to fill the containers with fresh water in the area. They were hoping there would be no more land. Bullock cart caravans continued forward. The carts had accompanied each other tightly. The chief led the caravan into town. Throughout the night, they continued their journey into the dark without realizing whether it was in the right direction or not.

At dawn, they realized they'd lost their way. After a long trip, they finally agreed to go back to the very same spot. As the caravan searched for the place, the sun was getting hotter. They finally reached the same spot where they had been the previous day. The water they brought given them has already been cast out. Already getting so hungry, they searched desperately for water but could not be found anywhere. The carts were stopped in a loop. They 'd died because of cold. Seeing no other option, Bodhisatva agreed to dig across the desert for water. He had been so determined he needed to drill a water well. But his quest continued in vain. Then he began searching for an suitable location where water could be discovered on digging. He went ahead, and discovered some cactus. It occurred to him that it was an appropriate place to dig, as cactus would not grow without underground water. He then told a cart owner, "Mate, dig over here. Water would possibly be found at this location."

He started digging. His spade hit a rock when he digged deep! He quit digging and yelled, "There's a block!" Bodhisatva saw the digger, and went down into the hole. He 'd moved back to the block. Suddenly its lights were glowing. Beneath the rock he could detect a rush of motion.

He went out of the pit then said to his companions, "If we don't do anything, we're sure to die of thirst. I've heard water running underneath the rock. Let's try to break the rock at any cost. We 're sure to get water. We're going to have power and courage. Let's try again with confidence." Bodhisatva was saddened to see that none of them had the bravery to go forward to search. Suddenly a young man stood up and managed to pick up the spade, and went down the pit. Seeing the Bodhisatva youth was optimistic for water. At last they found the water in the desert. The youth started to strike the stone with all his strength and the destroyed and a small, pleasant water fountain came up. Seen this, the crowds ran toward the fountain and started joyfully dancing. They quenched hunger. Bulls were given water, too. Both of them praised Bodhisatva, and went on their way. They soon reached the town. Thus Bodhisatva could save the lives of his friends with his courage and determination. In addition, the water fountain was a spot for the tourists to quench their thirst and relax. Strength and bravery is the key to success.

2.32 The Miser and his Gold

Once upon a time there was a Miser, at the foot of a hill, who used to conceal his gold in his backyard. He used to go around grinding it out every week and gloating about his earnings. A shooter went and found the gold with it, then fled. The next time the Miser gloated over his riches, none but the empty space was found. He tore his head and created an uproar that gathered around him all the neighbors, telling them how he used to come to see his income. "Have you ever pulled any of these out?" And one of them asked. "Nay," he responded, "I just came to look at it." "So come back and look at the spot," said a relative, "that's going to do you about as much good."

2.33 The Fox without Tail

It happens when a Fox trapped his tail in a net and losing all accept the stub in trying to set him safe. He was initially terrified of showing up alongside his fellow foxes. Yet eventually he decided to overcome his failure with a bolder approach and called all the foxes to a general meeting to address a proposal that he wanted to bring before them. The Fox said they'd both do away with their tails before they'd aembled. As their opponents, the puppies, confronted them, he found out how inconvenient a tail was; how often it was in the way as they wanted to settle down and have a nice conversation with each other. He had failed to see any gain from carrying such a pointless load. "That's all very well," said one of the older foxes;

"but I think you wouldn't have begged us to give up on our top ornament if you didn't skip yours."

2.34 Belling the Cat

Years after, the mice organized a general council to determine what action they should take to extricate their common foe, the Rat. Others said that, and others said that; so a young mouse actually got up and stated he had a proposal to make, and he decided he was going to follow. "We will all accept," he added, "that our biggest fear is if we are secretly and deceptively threatened by the adversary. So, if we could get a alert about her arrival, we might certainly stop her. I therefore assume that a tiny bell should be procured and fastened around the Cat's neck with a chain. Through that we will all realize where she was and be able to easily run while she was in the neighborhood. "When an old mouse got up and spoke, this proposal met with general excitement," that's all very good, but who is going to bell the cat? "The mice looked at each other and nobody spoke. Then the old mouse said:" It's simple to propose impossible solutions.

2.35 The Hare and the Tortoise

The Hare once bragged about its speed to the other birds. "I've never been defeated before," he said, "since I pushed my maximum force forward. I'm welcoming everybody here to play with me." Silently, the Tortoise replied, "I appreciate your challenge." "It's a nice one," said the Hare, "I might race all the way through you." Stop the appreciation before you harm me, "said the Tortoise. The Hare dropped out of reach at first, but then halted and laid down to take a nap and demonstrate his contempt for the Tortoise. The Tortoise plodded on and plodded on, and when the Hare woke up from his sleep, he noticed the Tortoise close to the winning post and could not catch up to avoid the race in time.

2.36 The Hare with many Friends

Like the other beasts a Hare was very popular, everyone claiming to be friends like her. And one day, she noticed the hounds coming with the aid of her many Parents, and wanted to hide. He then went to the horse, and asked him to save her from the hounds on her tail. However, he declined, claiming he had a important job to do for his boss. Instead she talked to the dog, hoping that he should repel the hounds from its ears. The bull responded, "I'm so sorry, but I've got a lady appointment, so I'm sure our goat buddy will do anything you want." Yet the goat worried that if he took her on it, his back would do any damage to her. He was sure that the horse was the best companion to converse with. Then she went to the ox, and then clarified to him the case. The ram replied: "My good friend, just another moment. I don't want to screw up on this occasion, since both sheep and hers are known to eat hounds. The Hare instead resorted to the calf as a last resort, lamenting that he was helpless to help her, because he did not want to see the responsibility on himself, since too many older people had rejected the task. By this time the hounds were very near, and the Hare took to her feet, and escaped narrowly.

2.37 The Lion, the Fox and the Beasts

As the Lion announced he was seriously sick and called the animals to come to hear his last Will and Testament. So the goat arrived at the Bear's den, and stayed a long time. A Sheep then went down, and a Calf came out to collect the final wishes of the God of the Beasts. Yet then the Lion started to heal, and came to the door of his den, finding the Cat, who had been waiting for some time outside. "Why don't you come over and show me your respects?" the Lion said to the Fox. "I ask Your Majesty's pardon," the Fox said, "but I find the tracks of the animals that have already come to you; and while I see some hoof-marks coming, I see none going back. I like remaining outside until those that got to your cave came out.

2.38 The Muleis Brains

The Lion and the Fox went to hunt together. At the advice of Fox the Lion gave the Mule a letter promising to reconcile their two communities. The Mule approached the meeting site, overjoyed at the prospect of a royal alliance. And when he entered the Lion just pounced on the Mule and said to the Fox: "Today's our dinner here. You watch it as I go and have a nap and you don't want and disturb my meal." The Lion went away and the Fox waited; then, noticing that his owner didn't come back, he went on to pick up the Mule's brains and chew them up. When the Lion came back, he soon remembered the lack of the brains and asked the Fox in a terrible voice: "What did you do for the brains?"You are Majestic, hearts! It had none, and it was never going to slip into your space.

2.39 The Milkmaid and her pail

A Milkmaid joined the market carrying her milk in a pail above her mouth. When she moved along she began planning what she was going to do with the money she was going to get for the milk. "I'm going to purchase some Farmer Brown fowls," she said, "and every morning they're going to lay eggs that I'm going to offer to the parson's wife. I'm going to buy a new dress and a new hat for myself with the money I get from the selling of these chickens, so when I go shop, all the young people won't come up to speak to me! Polly Shaw's going to be so mad ... but I don't matter. All I am trying to do is look at her and turn my head that direction. When she sang, she leaned her head back, the Pail came down, and all of the milk was poured free. Then she needed to go home and tell her mother what was going on. "Ah, kid," said mom. "Don't count the chickens until they're born."

2.40 The Cat-Maiden

The gods had previously challenged the likelihood that a living being could change its life. Zeus replied, "Absolutely," but Venus replied, "No." Then Zeus turned a Cat into a Maiden to check the matter, and then offered it to a bride to a young man. The service had been properly concluded, and the young people settled down for the wedding feast. "See," Zeus asked Venus, "how she's behaving even more. Who might tell yesterday she's just a mouse? Obviously it's shifting her nature?" Venus responded, "Wait a minute, and let the room loose a rat. The wife no longer noticed this until she decided to pounce on the animal. "You see, Indeed," said Venus.

2.41The Buffoon and the Countryman

At a country fair, there was a Buffoon that rendered the entire participants chuckle by imitating the cries of different animals. He wound up behaving so much like a donkey that he'd been hidden by the fans. Then a Countryman stood by said: "Sign a pig's squeak! Something likes that. You're taking me till tomorrow so I'm going to show you what it's like. The audience cheered but the countryman came on stage the next day, sure enough, so began squealing his head down so hideously that the people hissed started hurling stones at him to make him quit." And you fools! "He was shaking."See what you hissed," he picked up a little pig whose ear he pinched to make it squeal the squeals.

2.42 The Fox and the Goat

In a terrible mistake a Fox falls into a deep well he couldn't come out of. A goat came by shortly after, and told the Fox what he was doing there. "Oh, you haven't heard that? "There's going to be a major shortage," the Fox said; "and I jumped down here to be sure I had water. And how don't you spill, too?" The goat thought the idea was fine and jumped into the well. Even by placing his foot on her long legs, the Fox easily jumped onto her back and managed to crawl to the bottom of the well. "Well said, buddy," said the Fox, "remember next time, 'Do not follow the advice of a individual in troubl

Magic Bedtime Meditation

A Collection of Bed Night Stories For Kids to Create Imagination Meditation, Help Fall Asleep Fast

By Anna Smith

Respective authors own all copyrights not held by the publisher.

The information herein is offered for informational purposes solely and is universal as so. The presentation of the information is without contract or any type of guarantee assurance.

The trademarks that are used are without any consent and the publication of the trademark is without permission or backing by the trademark owner. All trademarks and brands within this book are for clarifying purposes only and are the owned by the owners themselves s, not affiliated with this document.

Chapter 1: Fiction Stories for Kids to Read at Bedtime

Any of the most famous books written for children aged 5-9 has great storylines, enjoyable sections of stories and fascinating details. Such books are also designed to help develop literacy skills and vocabulary competencies. Kids at these ages are usually between kindergarten and third grade, and even at this early age their reading skills differ, their passion for storytelling doesn't. The only thing you can do is find some imaginative stories that match the children's tastes and the desire to read. A fantasy children's novel tells the story from the author's point of view, who also serves as the main character at times. The reader can connect with this person by his or her feelings, gestures and emotions. The plot is about a child and generally adults play minor roles, if any. The plots of the story are simple, and usually a lesson or moral is presented.

1.1. A Chocolate Plane

Just around your age, Christiana is just a little girl. She's got pretty flowing brown hair and beautiful green eyes. She lives with her father in an apartment complex in the US city of Cambridge, Massachusetts. She is really beautiful. In fact, if you met her I think you'd like her. Perhaps she'd like you too and maybe you'd become great pals. One day Christiana decided to go to her room and read a really nice book right after dinner as she was reading it. That day, chocolate mousse cake was there for dessert. Christiana wanted to take hers into her room instead of sitting down and eating it at the dining table while her parents were talking. In reality, the cake Christiana brought into her room was not just a slice cut from a bigger cake. Instead, it was a beautiful, round, full cake. It was tiny, but bigger than a cupcake, for her and all. It had very delicious-looking chocolate frosting on the edges, with shapes of chocolate squiggle. This even had a strange pattern on top which wasn't really obvious when you looked closely.

While in her bed Christiana lost herself in reading her book-and forgot about the chocolate cake. She really didn't know when it was bedtime, but I think I should have. She actually didn't feel very thirsty. Instead, she just brushed her teeth, climbed into her room, turned the light out and cuddled up with her beloved fluffy animal, a cute orange and white cat called Amy. She then went to sleep. It's been several days before Christiana still remembered her chocolate cake. The cake was sitting on her shelf when she left, right as she first put it. She said-" Oh yes, that's going to be boring now. What a shame; that sounded so sweet! "But it didn't look old as she looked closer-in fact it still looked pretty fresh and tasty. That couldn't have been right!

Christiana took down the cake from the shelf and gave a quick swipe with her finger to the frosting only to get a little of sample.

There was no frosting left. "Oh, no!" It's stalemate! "She was listening. Yet she did a second, tougher lick at the frosting, just to make sure. None again-not even a little piece of frosting to sample. Perhaps by some miracle the cake inside was already fresh? (She was hungry this time.) She pushed hard on the unusual pattern at the top of the cake to find out. Then her finger appeared to crack straight through the strange pattern on the frosting chocolate and fall back into what seemed like the dark vacuum of outer space. Then it was on the floor again immediately and there was absolutely no trace on the cake. That was pretty weird!

1.2. Emergency in Catania

Until Christiana had time to talk about the puzzle a lot, the cake started adding a lot of bigger puzzles for her to worry about. This had begun to rock quite alarmingly. Then it increased in size and began to change shape-until suddenly it had turned into a gorgeous chocolate-filled airplane! The plane was so large it would hardly fit into her room. The plane's tail nearly hit her room frame, the nose leaned up against her window, and the wings extended straight from one side of her room all the way to the other side.

Ok, Christiana was shocked! This is a fairly ordinary response, you must admit. In fact, I'm going to bet you'd be amazed too if you had been the same thing. Yet you have certainly not had a similar encounter-at least, not yet. Only then Christiana found that the side that was near her height had a passenger door on it. The door swung open as soon as she saw it, and her cat Amy, clad in a light pink stewardess' uniform with gold buttons down the front, stood in the doorway and politely told her to go in. Of reality, Amy was talking cat language, but for some purpose what she said to Christiana was completely understandable. That might have been that, if you love someone a lot, you can hear what they're thinking even though they're not speaking out very plainly.

Okay, what would you do if you begged your beloved stuffed animal to jump into a chocolate plane that hadn't been in your house for a moment? Christian's father have always told her not to go in with a stranger in a car. But Amy, of course, wasn't an intruder. Nevertheless, Christiana said "No, thank you," only to be on the safe place.

The chocolate plane quickly vanished and the cake was gone! Once again Amy was a stuffed toy on the bed where Christiana still put her up in the morning. In reality, it was all back the way it had been before. Christiana, confused, started to think, "Am I really dreaming all this? "Still, she gently placed the chocolate cake back on her shelf for some reason, instead of tossing it out into the oven. She chose not to say what had happened, either. Nobody's believe it! In reality, she chose not to believe it either.

Believe that, do you? Perhaps tonight you will think about it, and then decide. I'll tell you a separate story about bedtime tomorrow.

Christiana awaked quite unexpectedly the next morning. Her beloved stuffed animal, Amy, stood by her bedside and shook her shoulder to wake her up. Christiana, without pausing to consider how odd it was, saw the anxious expression on Amy's face and said immediately, "Amy, what's wrong? "Amy, using cat talk, began explaining an interesting story to Christiana.

"Christiana," she said, "two years ago, your parents took you to spend a couple of months in Australia, remember? The building you lived in was just by the ocean's coast at Coo gee. (Coo gee is a strange word for a place, I know. It means something like 'Stinky Seaweed' in an Aboriginal language, but when we were there it wasn't at all smelly.) Our Catania Rescue Team saw you picking up the Kittens and then heard what your Mother said. They were really shocked you saw the kittens at all, and your mom could see them as well. The cats living in Catania can only be seen by a few, a unique humans. Even the Rescue Squad was careful to let you take the Kittens to the vet. Often the vets are going to determine the cats are too ill to heal and have to be put to sleep, so we didn't want that.

I clarified that you were a very unique human being, and that we should have faith in you. I said I knew you very well when I was born-I was your most special cat ever. I told them you loved cats intensely. I always said you had incredible Cat Magical abilities you didn't even know about. With Christiana as the mother of the Kitten, I was confident that no doctor would ever contemplate putting our Kittens to sleep. I was confident that the unique CatMagical abilities of Christiana and the vet's drugs would heal the Kittens.

So, you know when you took the Kittens to the doctor, and she gave them some medication. You carried the Kittens home after that, and took good care of them. You know the Kittens were much happier when they began running in the house and chasing one another!

After the six Kittens got absolutely healthy, your Mom immediately couldn't see them anymore. She thought they ran! It shocked you, because you could see them clearly still. (I had to say why a Catlandia Citizen Cat can only be heard by average people because it needs to be seen. Your mom has been able to see the Kittens when they were ill and they had to be noticed.

You took the six Kittens back to Catlandia the next day, and released them where you found them. We were both very pleased to see them again, and relieved to see them back to safety. These Kittens have grown up now, and are Catlandia 's adult cat residents. We fondly remember you and always go by the names you give them when you were younger and Kittens.

In truth, every one of us kindly remembers you for your very good deed.

"There was a wide park next to your home, with grass and pretty huge rocks. On sunny days, on the way down the very steep hill to the beach you can stroll through that park. Often you'd note to your father or mother that there appeared to be a lot of cats running around in the park. Your mother and dad did not seem to know what you said-they saw no cats. You thought they were behaving like other grown-ups, being unobservant.

"You have found that all of us were pretty stunning and elegant on our fur and had many different designs. I have to remind you now that, at times, when you didn't have me with you, I wasn't on your pillow where you put me every morning. I was one of those cats that you saw in the park playing! "(When she said that last part, Amy blushed a little. She didn't want Christiana to think she was pregnant or to think about herself as especially stunning.

"One day ... Remember? -- Six newborn Kittens were discovered next to a rock with no mother to care for. They were very ill and they were very thirsty. Our Catlandia Emergency Team have heard, and when you stopped by we were about to take the Kittens to Catlandia Hospital. You scooped all the Kittens up into your arms as soon as you saw them, and asked your mom if you should take them home to nurse them back to safety. Your mom was afraid they might catch it, but at last she said "Yep.

Still, before you can carry them along, we will send the Kittens to a veterinarian for a checkup.

1.3. Flying to Catlandia

She did not know what to think as Christiana walked through the doorway and onto the Chocolate Aircraft. It was eight gorgeous seats that she noticed, set in two rows, one on either side of the aircraft. There were clearly 3 seats on the left side made just for pets and then one on its front made for a human. In reality, that one seemed to be made only for Christiana because, as she saw to her shock now, on the back she had her name written in gold. There were four more pet seats on the right hand side.

With her pink dress flight crew, Amy immediately welcomed Christiana to her seat and assisted tighten her seatbelt. Instead Amy sat in the front cat seat, fastening her own seatbelt for takeoff. (Just in case you've never seen a cat airplane seat before, I would note it's pretty much like a perfectly lined cat bed with sides. You should jump in (if you're a pet) and then extend the safety harness over the top and tighten it for safety.)

As soon as they were settled, the plane took off with no mess at all. One moment Christiana could see her familiar bedroom outside of the plane's windows, and the next moment the plane was soaring into the air - and then it began to go very quickly forward. When the plane was underway and the seatbelt sign was turned off, Amy opened her belt, rose from her place, and came over to Christiana. Would you like a snack, she said? "Well, yes thank you" said Christiana. "What do you have?" "Chocolate cake and chocolate milk." "Wonderful! I would like some please." The food was delicious - dark chocolate was Christiana's favorite, and the plane had just the right kind. The Catlandia Airlines plane continued to fly silently at high speed for several hours, across land and water. At first Christiana wanted to warn Amy about the Catlandia situation, but Amy would only say "You have to warn the Acting Chief Cat about it" and then she would look really sad and concerned. Christiana wanted to rub Amy underneath her ears to calm her down-that's what she normally did when Amy got upset. Yet she wasn't so confident whether biting a flight attendant wearing a pink dress and gold buttons behind the ears would be acceptable behavior. So she was content with looking out the window. For a while, the view of the clouds was fascinating but then, I must confess, it got pretty dull. And when the plane actually began to descend Christiana was relieved. "We're landing at Catlandia Airport," Amy said, "And tighten your seatbelt, and keep your seatback straight."

Christiana now discovered that the new chief Cat had arrived to Catlandia Airport with a large group of Catlandia Citizen Cats to meet with her. They were both looking very nervous and pointing towards the Catlandia border with their hands.

Christiana pointed at where they were referring and immediately grasped the issue without having any clarification. Catlandia was encircled by bulldozers! Each was employed by a driver and they were obviously waiting for Catlandia to drive in and straighten! The Acting Chief Cat has explained that they are working to develop park seaside residences. (Know that Catlandia was situated in a park on the seaside of the Australian city of Coogee? Naturally, many people enjoy living on the seaside-maybe you do too. As you can realize, that made the park a very attractive place to build more housing.)

The people wanting houses could not be held responsible, of course. After all, they did not have the idea that Catlandia was magical and unique to cats. However, very obviously something had to be done right away! Christina turned to the new Chief Cat and said: "What steps are you going to take? The Acting Chief Cat just gazed at her and said - "I have no idea! But I am not anxious, because we in Catlandia believe that you will know how to "Save the Day!"

Well-Christiana wasn't getting the faintest notion what to do. Yet it was only then that the bulldozers engines began, and she obviously needed to do something-but what? Ok, I have to admit, this is a definite urgency! I'm sad to admit I have really no idea what to do next with Christiana. Are you? Okay, when we next think about Christiana's exploits, we'll learn what happens. This is the time to go to relax. Sweet dreams to you!

1.4. Christiana Saves the Day

Notice there were bulldozers circling Catlandia in our last story? It had been told the bulldozer drivers to flatten the seaside park so that people could build apartments by the ocean. The drivers seemed to have no idea Catlandia would flatten too. Catlandian Citizen Animals, if you know, are blind to anyone other very unique individuals. In fact Christiana was the only human who knew that there was Catlandia!

Can you still recall Christiana was asked by the Acting Chief Cat that he has no idea what to can with this emergency? He said, though, that he was certain Christiana would save the day. Then he began kissing the back of his paws and relaxing peacefully. Christiana sadly didn't have the slightest idea of what to do. Just then the bulldozers' engines started and the vehicles began clinging toward Catlandia's precious boundaries. Clearly Christiana must have done it instantly!

Suddenly Christiana found one of her Cat Magical abilities, without preparing it. In her mind center began to form an image of a beautiful pink rose. She felt her interest pulled intensely towards it and as she focused on it, a very light pink started to shine. (Possibly if anything happened to you the flower would have a different hue, but pink was the favorite color of Christiana.)

The glowing flora in her mind glowed gradually until it was very bright. Suddenly the Cats that looked on could see the glow too. It appeared to overshadow Christiana, at first. Instead, each of them started to extend and reach. As it did, they penetrated their minds with the image of Christiana's pink rose and their minds joined Christiana's to further enhance its light. All watched with amazement as the glow moved out to Catlandia's borders. To Christiana and Catlandia's watching people, they now all seemed to be inside a stunning, sparkling pink bowl that totally surrounded Catlandia.

Little attention was paid by the bulldozer drivers to the vivid pink light in front of them as they attempted to advance over barriers and into Catlandia. Then they discovered that the glow somehow prevented them from pushing forward altogether. And the strongest computers have been unable to push forward. Okay, to some of the staff, it made little sense. Of that matter, Christiana and the Catlandian Citizen Cats didn't make any sense either. But it seemed to succeed and they kept focused on Christiana's stunning pink rose-and the bulldozers stayed totally surrounded. The bulldozer drivers eventually, profoundly confused, went home for the night.

Oh, it is hard work for a young girl to push off bulldozers-including one with CatMagical powers. Amy, who had much love for Christiana and loved her very well, obviously understood that Christiana was tiring. Christiana could rest until morning, but Amy knew the drivers would definitely be back with even more efficient machines in the morning. So, she talked to the Acting Chief Cat as a matter of urgency who spoke with others. An emergency call went out to all Citizen Cats in Catlandia to come to Catlandia Airport for Christiana's assistance immediately. Everyone had arrived, of course. Young and old Catlandian people, including the smallest Kittens, flooded to Catlandia Airport all night long. They were all keen to help Christiana save Catlandia in her war. As Amy had feared, the puzzled drivers returned in the morning and brought some very powerful machines along. The employees have started their bulldozers once again after getting coffee. Christiana and the cats easily again focused in Christiana's mind on the pretty pink rose, and again produced the softly shining bowl over Catlandia. At a sound, all the devices started pressing in at once toward all the headland sides of the shining pink pot. Under the leadership of Christiana all Catlandian Citizen Cats focused hard to preserve the glow in place. Suddenly a sharp crack happened! The rough driving of the bulldozers had already driven Catlandia some miles from the mainland-Catlandia had been a peninsula! Everybody was shocked by the abrupt outcome-including Bulldozer drivers and Catlandia people. What occurred next, though, was much more surprising. Catlandia clearly and immediately disappeared from human vision without a sound! So far as the construction workers could hear, there was now a new seashore where Catlandia's borders had just been a moment before! What they saw right in front of their machines was a steep cliff, with only the ocean beyond. They had clearly to avoid trying to move on. They didn't want their machines to go down into the sea after all!

Well, I think you would agree with me that all of this is very weird. Please don't worry though. I assure you it isn't really gone Catlandia. I also inform you that Christiana and Catlandia's Resident Cats were very healthy while they were quite shocked. Now go to sleep gently. Perhaps in a dream you will find an answer to the mystery. If not, I'll explain precisely what happened in our next story at bedtime.

1.5. Mystery Solved

Ok, from our last bedtime story, you'll note that the bulldozers of the staff had driven so hard at Catlandia's boundaries that it unexpectedly split away from Australian Mainland and became a peninsula. Around the same time what was once Catlandia Island has suddenly and absolutely vanished from Humans' vision!

Christiana and the Resident Cats of Catlandia had no clue of what had just transpired in the first moment since Catlandia broke apart. One moment they worked intensely on helping to enhance the light of Christiana's CatMagical pink rose. The next moment they all tumbled around from the jolt separating Catlandia from the mainland. The jolt disrupted their attention too, of course, and the bright pink boll the sheltered Catlandia from the bulldozers had collapsed completely.

Christiana and Amy first discovered this, and they expected the worst. No, no! Were the bulldozers crossing the frontiers? But when they looked up to see what the Humans were doing, they were amazed to see that all the drivers had stepped out of their workstations and were just staring! They were looking at what on earth? Had the Catlandian Citizens suddenly become visible? No, it didn't feel that way-the Humans didn't really look at them directly. Instead they all appeared to head in different directions.

Christiana told the cats around her to raise their tails and meow and see if they could draw any attention and make sure the Humans did not see them. The adult cats did exactly what she requested, right away. I have to tell you, though, that a few of the fairly young cats took this opportunity to be rather impolite. Some began to make faces at the humans. Some even pressed their paws against their mouths, making very grim noises! (I 'm sure you'd never do that!) If the Humans didn't respond, Amy and the Acting Chief Cat of Catlandia realized they were still all very invisible-that was a great relief!

But why did the bulldozer drivers suddenly stop trying to push across the frontiers of Catlandia? The Chief Geologist in Catlandia was the one who actually solved the mystery. (A geologist, if you wonder, is someone who knows a great deal about the earth and the rocks and islands and the like.) She noticed the break in the land at the border and quickly realized that Catlandia was now an island. She also knew that Christiana and the Cats were still invisible to humans, largely through the impolite efforts of the Kittens. Her next thought was the secret to mystery solving. When Catlandia was an island, she concluded, what must have changed is that each Resident Cat's human CatMagical invisibility abilities had unexpectedly started escaping to the mainland outside of Catlandia's borders. What would happen if all the force of invisibility existed within Catlandia? This will suffice to make Catlandia's whole (rather small) island instantly as invisible as the Cat Citizens themselves! This was it!

Which was the Puzzle Solution!

The Chief Geologist was able to explain her idea to the Acting Chief Cat-who agreed and then immediately declared it to all Catlandian people. There was tremendous happiness straight away! All the worries about Catlandia seemed to be resolved suddenly!

Of course, maybe you thought Catlandians didn't have any worries aside from the very urgent matter of the bulldozers I told you about. In reality, there is still something to think about when humans and cats share the same dwelling ground. For starters, on their way to Coogee Beach, humans frequently strolled through the park. But, of course, as we know, the park was also Catlandia, although that was not known to the Humans. A human crossing the park would sometimes suddenly travel across an invisible Catlandian Citizen Cat. That really happened quite frequently as Citizen Cats always took their afternoon snoozes on the dry, sunlit paths of the park. That was obviously nobody's fault. (Certainly, it couldn't be blamed for the Cats. As everyone knows, a warm, sunlit pavement is just too tempting!) But a collision could hurt both humans and cat. Now, at least, Catlandans no longer had to think about these things-they had their very own island country completely to themselves for the first time! The best part was that no human knew it was there-although it was only three feet away, really!

The Catlandians celebrated their new independent Island Nation for several hours, frolicking in the grass and meowing with great joy! The younger Kittens of course starting jumping on each other, looking for a good surprise. Some even risked jumping just for fun at the older cats. Over all, they were all too pleased to advise them to mind their manners please! Then, quite unexpectedly, they all turned their attention to Christiana again! She was the one who had led them to save Catlandia in their surprising, successful effort! She was the actual founder of their new Island Nation and a heroine! At a signal from the Acting Chief Cat, all of the Citizen Cats quickly organized themselves into two long lines along the path leading from Catlandia Airport to Catlandia Center (which was not too far away actually).

Leaders of the Celebrations Team then walked along the lines passing out mouse-shaped noisemakers to everyone.

A procession was then formed at the front with Christiana and Amy as well as the acting leader cat. As all the Catlandia Citizen Cats cheered wildly and blowing on their noisemakers they marched along the road. Needless to add, Christiana thanked their thanks. Nevertheless, she blushed many times to the roots of her deep brown hair as she walked down the road towards Catlandia's Royal Palace.

Upon finally arriving at the Residence, they ascended the grand staircase, bowed one last time to the audience, and entered. The crowds swiftly went home for the night after that. Everyone was after all very weary of everything they had been through. Of course, Christiana was especially exhausted, so as soon as the new chief Cat took her to a room, she washed her face so paws, brushed her teeth (there was a pretty new toothbrush laid out again for her), said good night to her father in her head and promptly fell into a deep sleep.

Now it's necessary to switch the light out, too, and go to sleep like Christiana. I'll remind you what happens next when we have a different story around bedtime. Nice dreams to you!

1.6. Christiana learns about her Royal Past

After a long and beautiful sleep in the morning Christiana joined Amy and the new chief Cat for a warm milk breakfast. The acting chief cat and Amy drank from beautiful saucers on their milk. Christiana drank her milk from a crystal glass decorated with Catlandia's Royal Crest, which the Palace Chef Cat had thoughtfully supplied.

While addressing the great activities of the day before, Christiana told the Acting Chief Cat if he and the other Catlandian Citizen Cats felt she was different and why they were so confident that she might support them in their time of need. The new lead cat then told an interesting story to Christiana. "Christiana," solemnly said the new chief Cat, "Now that you have started to discover your CatMagical Powers, you also need to learn about your Royal History. You can also understand why we invited you to come to Catlandia after you understand this history, and why we knew beyond doubt that you would Save the Day.

Let me start by saying that many humans somewhere in their family trees have magical Cat qualities. No Cat knows why, and humans are completely unaware of that. Humans will, of course, say things sometimes that should give them a hint. They might say, for example: "When Uncle George laughs, he just looks like the Cat that ate the Canary! "Or they could say, 'Aunt Edna is walking with an incredible grace of Catlike! "(Amy blushed a little at this moment. She wasn't proud, but deep in her heart she knew she walked with incredible Catlike elegance. Of course, Amy was a Cat, so maybe we shouldn't be too surprised by that.)

In any case, most humans inherit very little from their parents in the form of magical Cat attributes. But on extremely rare occasions, attributes from ancestors of a Person will be mixed in such a way that a Human child will be born with very powerful CatMagical forces!

When an infant is born somewhere in the world with very powerful CatMagical abilities, we learn about it immediately in Catlandia. I don't know why, but I know that since the day you were born, all of Catlandia's Resident Cats have been aware of your CatMagical abilities. This is so even though we live in Australia and you were raised in America far from us.

As I said, kids like you are precious and very rare. Indeed the last child born over 200 years ago with powers like yours! Throughout Catlandia's long history, humans with CatMagical powers have been saving the day when Catlandia was in danger.

That is why I was so confident yesterday that you could save us somehow. And, you have to admit you have really rescued us in the most beautiful and unexpected way!

When the Acting Chief Cat finished speaking Christiana became absolutely speechless. She said at last: But I am totally human- I am not an Animal! Of course, I love Cats and I love Amy in particular but I don't want to be a Cat! I just don't want to be part of Pet! (Then she turned to Amy and begged forgiveness if she had hurt her, but Amy said that she knew it completely. After all, she liked to be a Cat and wouldn't even want to be part of a Human!)

"Christiana, possessing CatMagical Abilities simply means you are a human being with an extraordinary ability to help Cats and all other living things when they are in danger or pain. It doesn't mean you're less human in any way. Indeed, I think a human being who can help other species in particular shows wonderful human qualities-do not you? "Amy, who listened carefully, enthusiastically nodded her head. Christiana was happy to agree, and afterwards felt much more comfortable with her CatMagical Powers.

The Acting Chief Cat spoke again after a pause to refill its saucer of milk. He said, "Christiana, did you ever wonder why my title is Chief Acting Cat?" "Christiana said she was wondering-a little bit. Christiana," he said, "I've got that title because I'm just acting as the ruler of Catlandia until you're old enough to have your Coronation and rule as the Queen of Catlandia! In fact you've got the title of Princess of Catlandia right now!

The Acting Chief Cat talked again after a break to empty its saucer of milk. He said, "Christiana, do you ever think why my title is Chief Acting Cat?" "Christiana said she was wondering-a little bit. Christiana," he said, "I've got that title because I'm just acting as the ruler of Catlandia until you're old enough to have your Coronation and rule as the Queen of Catlandia! In truth you've got the title of Princess of Catlandia right now!

Christiana was so shocked! "Me, a Catalan princess?! How breathtaking! "

With eager approval, Amy shook her head once more. That would be great! There could be special rights for the pet Cat of the Queen, after all! Catnip's might be huge bowls every day? Christiana too had a daydream. "Wait just for my friends to hear this! I should ask them to live in the Castle! There will be no parents allowed to! We will sit up the entire evening! We should learn to make a living like Animals! Will cats go to school? Maybe not!!!!?..."

Christiana unexpectedly had a concern. "If I'm a Catalan princess, doesn't that mean my father and mother are the King and Queen of Catlandia? No," the acting chief cat said, "your parents are not the queen and the king. Royal Catlandian Titles only belong to those with very strong CatMagical abilities-it has little to do with human families. Indeed, after this visit to

Catlandia, when you return to your home, you will find that you are the only one who knows that Catlandia exists! For our health, the secrecy is important. If humans knew of Catlandia they'd like to study us. Or they could find oil beneath our land and ask us to move, or something like that. Often, humans are very nice to cats, but sometimes they can be difficult too.

"Just wait," Christiana said, pondering whether she could be supposed to keep this secret. "Is this not to say to my friends? Would be awesome to tell them I am a princess! "When Christiana again managed to pay attention to what the Acting Chief Cat was saying, she found he was saying that she could of course invite her friends to the Palace for sleepwalks-after all, it was her Palace-but that after her friends had gone home they would remember nothing of the visit or of Catlandia. They wouldn't remember she was a princess either. But the nice thing was, he said, that she would be shocked all over again every time she welcomed them to Catlandia and showed them she was a queen!!

Oh, Christiana did have more concerns, of course. Can she say Catlandia about her parents? "Alas not," was the comment. Should she live at home anyway? "Naturally" was the reaction. Because the Acting Chief Cat would be able to manage things in her absence, she could stay anywhere she wanted. When an emergency occurred in Catlandia he would always inform her. She must hurry back to her Kingdom on those occasions to assist her Faithful Suet's. As you might guess, there were plenty of questions and answers. Learning how to be a Princess at once isn't easy! I'm sure we're going to hear more about it in future bedtime stories but not now.

By the way, I just want to ask you a question before you go to sleep. Do you think you might have some CatMagical Abilities that you don't already know about? Do you feel a great fondness for Cats, for starters, that you really cannot explain? If so, this could be a hint that someday you'll develop CatMagical Powers! Anyway, just in case, it could be worth dreaming about. Sweet dreams to you!

1.7. Christiana tours Catlandia City

You can recall that the Acting Chief Cat announced to Christiana that she was Princess Christiana of Catlandia in reality during our last bedtime story! He also said she would become Queen some day when she was older! You can recall after the incredible news there was a lot of debate about the rules for becoming a princess. The talk had literally continued till well after lunch! All this was of course very important, but also a little dull!

The acting lead cat could see that with all the serious conversation Christiana had grown sick. And he politely wondered if she'd like a little stroll before dinner through Catlandia City Centre. It might be fun for her to see a little more of her Country, he said. Christiana agreed, and they strolled down to the Grand Staircase and began walking down to the beautiful road below. So soon so Princess Christiana could be heard from below, three great Meows had gone up from the thousands of Catlandia Citizen Cats who had gathered there! Christiana was shocked but Acting Principal Cat and Amy were both laughing. We were in on the game! When Christiana overtook her astonishment and looked closer, she found that in the Royal Colors of Catlandia (Light Pink and Gold) her people had made banners and flags, the backdrop of each banner was light pink and the gold was used to spell out "Long live Princess Christiana! "On all flags and banners. This was a fantastic experience! Almost every Cat had two flags, one in each paw and raised them madly! Each building had large banners draped over the front. For her honor, all the roads were painted purple! Christiana blushed as she saw that it was all about her. But the subjects of Cat land's Resident Cat looked so relaxed she soon became really relaxed too! She felt very proud of herself too. She had just saved the day yesterday! Maybe someday she will grow to become a wise and pure Empress, and truly deserving of the respect of her people. She'd done the hardest! Meanwhile, she had started to get a strong feeling that being Queen of Catlandia might really be fun!

When Christiana visited Catlandia's Capital City she began to learn more about how her Citizen Cats lived. She had most of her subjects living in Tree Towers.

This looks a little like the cat furniture that you usually see in pet shops, except more

They were a lot heavier, of course. -- Tree Tower was like a flagpole, a long upright pole, which was as tall as a large tree. But, unlike trees, for fast climbing each one was covered in green and brown carpeting. The colors made the Tree Towers to blend in beautifully with the actual Catlandia City trees.

Platforms in bright colors like fruit or flowers were tied to the branches of each Tree Tower. This were the apartments for the cat. Everyone had a scratching carpeted pad, a big Storage Chest for cat toys, and all the other stuff that cats need to have a nice home. Thanks to the wide open driveways in front of the platforms, kittens and adults could only walk onto the porch and meow each other anytime they wished. Even the most daring Kittens could see each other by leaping straight from site to site, rather than scaling the central carpeted pole like the adults did. (Of course, the kittens had to be careful not to leap straight on top of someone by accident. So if they did, they had to make sure to say "excuse me" very politely. Perhaps your parents told you to say "excuse me" even if you fall on someone unpredictably?)

There were all the other items that Catlandia Citizen Cats wanted more out of the City Centre. There were stunning fields with neatly tended Catnip crops. There were pretty rows of fishing poles by the cliff-side where Catlandia ended at sea, that everyone could borrow to catch a good fish for dinner. There were also beautiful Cat-parks with special systems where Kittens could practice leaping from high heights, navigating with their tails and landing on their paws. That was sounding nice. Christiana wondered a bit, whether she should still try to land on her feet even though she didn't have a tail. One day, she vowed to pursue it. All in all, Christiana considered Catlandia Resident Cats happily lived together comfortably and peacefully. That was nice to hear. The Acting Chief Pet, Christiana and Amy returned to the Palace after walking much of the day, and ascended the Grand Staircase again. Then they had a wonderful meal for the Cats, with air-dried grasshoppers and timothy grass spiced with catnip, and she had cheese and catnip cake. After dinner had finished, Amy said it would be time to go to bed. After all, they had not stopped to take a Cat Nap all day, as she pointed out! Come to think about it, it's time for you, Little One, to go to bed too! We'll have another story about bedtime really soon!

Chapter 2: Stories for Sleep Meditation & Stimulating Mindfulness

To raise your kid's mindfulness, stories do help. It's an essential part of sleep meditation to tell you children such stories that improve their mindfulness

2.1 What you want to reap only Grow

A grandpa and his grandson sat on a sandstone in the sunlight next to a blabbering river. "Say me one tale," the grandchild said. "It is a two-wolf saga," granddad replied. "As we evolve it often seems like 2 wolves are seeking to take influence within us. The very first wolf of fluffy grey fur, a loving look in his eye, and perhaps even a big grin on his lips, you can picture. It is a wolf who seldom bars his dentures and seems to be ready to step back and let nourish the other little ones. We could name him the wolf of harmony, compassion and goodness, for the wolf believes that if we can live with each other in harmony, every creature or every individual beings will be much satisfied. "Love is better to this wolf than any other. You see, she thinks our people and animals existence will stop existing lacking compassion. It was because a mother loves her child that she takes care of her, cooks her, dresses her, covers her and saves her from danger. We came into this world as an act of compassion and we evolve through the love parents give us.

As we value and are cherished in exchange, we long to be cherished, and the lives are nourished and filled. "Apparently the wolf also knows that compassion is portion of that love. While we are compassionate to someone they are apt to show compassion back to us, but not always. Grin at somebody and they will smile back with a fair chance. Go off to be beneficial and the one you are helpings more effective to assist you when you really need it. Wolves are a little like people, and reside in groups. They blend together, and usually feel happier if they mix in a dry, tactful way. "But," the grandfather added, "Let's say that the pack includes another wolf that doesn't believe the same things.

This wolf does have a really imply, mischievous face. Sometimes it backs away its lips to threatening manner ignore its teeth toward other living creatures. Generally they sense terror more than love and reverence as it happens, for this is the wolf of anger, greed and hate. Maybe it's afraid or nervous, and so it's just on watch. Unfortunately, it hasn't realized that it creates a lot of negative emotions among itself and in the other wolves by being too frustrated or hostile to others, by thinking about who and what it opposes instead of whom or what it enjoys.

This wolf is out for amount one, while wolf of peace, compassion, and goodness sout for the joy well-being of everyone else, as well as their own. "As you may guess, there could be 2 such wolf in a team fighting to determine May one is heading off on its way. The wolf of peace, love, and compassion likes to give those principles with all, but the wolf of anxiety, covetousness, and hate appears to care only for himself. It feels terrible about itself and leaves it feeling bad for the others. "Let us begin to believe," the grandfather said, "that there are two these wolves in a fight inside you."

The little boy, wide-eyed, gazed up at his grandparents. "Who's looking to dominate? "He inquired anxiously. The grandfather generally frowned, compassion in his eyes, gentleness in his expression, replying, "Whichever you serve."

2.2 Changing modes of Attitude

For almost as long as Danny could recall gulls had perched on the staircase of his building's window ledge since he's a tiny kid. It may have been because his mother and father always put bits of their uneaten food out to feed the gulls.

When Danny was very small, he was afraid of the gulls. And the gulls trembled at him. Whenever the birds moved by, he was terrified that they would peck him and suddenly brought away. The gulls flew swiftly when he walked, too. They were both terrified and so both stayed away apart from one another don't think there was a pivotal moment where Danny Unexpectedly started fearing the gulls, or the gulls started fearing Danny. Perhaps they were only getting a bit more use to it.

Mother could keep out Danny's hand with a slice of bread as they did, defending this from a sneering nibble. Danny was astonished by how softly it was taken by the birds — anything that he would not have learned had he permitted his dread to conquer. He started to feel somewhat more convinced to keep out a piece of meat with himself when he realized this and the gulls were a little more willing to try and collect it, softly. As he had expected, this tall, floppy snout is not used to hurt him. As his mom explained, her beak was rolled up in one like his fingers and lips. He used it to slowly pluck the food from under his Fingertips, much like he could use his fingertips to pick something delicate. I'm not sure if anyone told him the magpies wouldn't hurt, he might have embraced it. It would be something he wanted to learn for himself, as it is with a great many things.

As he started to serve the gulls, he learnt regarding them. And stuff about himself. Initially he assumed that gulls were gulls. He had not even pretty much stopped and realize their distinctions. How much he saw may have been restricted by his worry. Any issues were clear as he started to pay note. He managed to identify the young males in their color schemes which were uniquely monochrome. They were wider than the women, with white and black trends flecking their backs. The younger folks were greyish and loud, squawking endlessly till food was jabbed down their necks, and then their relentless squawking does seem to pause just lengthy enough just to consume the meals so when they started pushing extra. Danny felt he wouldn't like to be a mummy magpie. Typically it was the largest and oldest person who came out first to drink.

Danny could recognize him for having a twisted knee with a pointy pile on it. Mom says she feels she might have destroyed it. Danny nicknamed him Peg-leg, for that explanation.

A day Danny told his mother, "I assure I can get peg legged on my hand and consume. I guarantee you probably won't," chuckled His wife, "you've not got the stamina. "Danny was calculated and he's even more determinated so if his mother said the same of his humility. He will also supply Peg-leg every day thereafter, retain the meat in his right side and holding his left hand, palms facing, here between food and the bird. Peg leg will either jump over his left hand at first, or float onto the other part of the staircase wall, escaping the hand of Danny. It would not be as quick as Danny had assumed, but he would not give up.

As he kept out the bread, he started looking up. It was that he didn't look at the gulls really anything important. The newer gulls did not even look as you staring after them when they came to have the milk. He screened it out: keep staring them in their eye sockets and maintain their discrepancy; arch your back away of your fingers & pick up the food. Everything you find is fascinating when you have the opportunity to be diligent and

Danny was quite, very careful, as much as his mother expected he should be. He'd be worrying about whether he'd lure Peg leg to consume out of his hand the night while riding his motorcycle to / from classes. Perhaps the hand was too near to his nose. He noticed that if he place himself in a magpie's place, then the forehead is the wrong position. So this is where their snout is, with which they assault. If they were struck by yet another creature, it will come from the nose. Probably Peg leg will feel better, as on his feet, away of Danny's nose. Danny sat in a chair, putting his feet on the railings of the verandah, extending his legs as far as he could allow them. He stuck out the meat to the end of his neck, then turned down. He wanted to watch, and did not have to discipline himself. It sure took effort, and Danny considered of offering many occasion.

And it has been few days since this happening. Peg leg jumped on the foot of Danny, stuck out his snout as far as he can possible, and scooped the meat from the fingertips of Danny. Danny stood by his arm and leg if they were already cold. Indeed his action was almost his only action. He started to move his hand nearer to his torso with each day, slowly but surely Peg leg just got somewhat pretty close.

Peg leg aren't a late thinkers, Danny figured. He is just afraid. He has to knowhow to believe me. I have to go slow, and allowed him built up his trust. Danny put the left hand on his thighs as he served his right to Peg leg. As Peg leg was used to stepping there with his left hand, this was only a short time until he climbed on Danny's back. The next move was hard but Danny gradually and carefully handled it. Danny managed to take it, ever so slowly, off his thigh with Peg leg balancing on his side but quickly jumped off. Danny wondered if he would ever get passed that place but, sure indeed, in period Peg leg will sit just a few centimeters over his thigh on Danny's side. There have been some many weeks and several more careful moves until one day Danny stepped over onto the back yard, putting his left hand in the air with some beef at his right. Peg leg swooped from a branch, falling right on the extended arm of Danny. Can you take a picture of how Danny would have felt? It has to be impossible to master that if you want to leap over the moon, you have to remain as still as a stone. Danny couldn't even scream for Mom to take a peek. Now with all the period they had spent to accept one another and he really don't want to scare Peg- leg. He wanted to figure out what it's like to be exhilarated while at the same times still calm, what it was like to love the experience. Of course, both Danny's mom and dad needed to know, but at first they didn't fully accept what they were seeing do think, occasionally, who come to understand more. Was it the family members of Danny, of Peg leg or of Danny?

2.3 In the Lime Light: A Doll's Story

There used to be a doll, a very lovely doll named Pollyrma the fourth. Pollyrma the fourth was really something, a custom built figurine that any buyer of gorgeous dolls would absolutely adore to have — apart from Pollyrma the fourth, her existing proprietors, which seemed very poor. Pollyrma the fourth therefore did not realize about herself as to be exceptional. She probably thought about herself as regular simple Dolly the Polly.

One nice afternoon Dolly the Polly landed herself in a bidding. Understand exactly what it's like? You should have seen competitions on television where so many persons choose to have the same stuff and that they all offer a better deal before they approve the highest bid.

Polly didn't really know how she came to get into this situation, and even if there was anything she had done anything wrong to land in here, she wondered several times. The sale kind of didn't seem fair, but nothing Polly could do to help avoid whatever was going on so it didn't make much sense either.

There was a guy in the middle of the room vying for Dolly the Polly. He looked to be a sweet, caring guy who really happened to adore her and also desire her to be around him in his house. There was a lady on the other corner of room who was competing for Polly too. She always looked gorgeous kindhearted, and was fully determined to get Dolly the Polly for her in her home. Since they all make an offer it seemed like Polly might hear them talking, "Step in with me and stay with me. I'll look after you. I'm going to watch out for you. I want you to be in my room. "If a doll looked upset, then sweet little Polly would look so sad. Since she'd felt uncomfortable. She usually won't like being stuck in the middle, she didn't actually know that what house to end up living in, probably wouldn't feel she seemed to have a lot of options and just doesn't really want to make that decision even if she'd had.

As the man was bidding on one corner and the woman was biding from the other, Dolly the Polly got wondering about substitutes. It was not fine, if both agree to be with each other and she could be around with them. She was self-talking. If this is not actually happening, or I could live portion of the time with one party, and rest of the time with the other. There might be a way to make everyone joyous.

In his offer the guy was louder. The lady got more anxious. Dolly the Polly begin to realize it might be safer if she slid off the window sill where she had been seen. If she was dented or damaged, perhaps the conflict could also halt for her. Then she noticed that everyone will be un- happy if that took place, even not Polly herself.

She suspected, why the person was becoming so noisy and the lady so anxious. Maybe it was as every one of them admired her so much because they assumed they could have been delighted if she were theirs alone? When Polly imagined of them cherishing her and seeking her, she felt a lot better. Whoever won and whoever she ended up living with, that was the thing which that will remain intact: that the lady & the gentle man were vying since they chose Polly, as she was different and beautiful so she was adored and remunerated.

Just what took place that day in the sale house, or the times earlier, or even the days to come, Dolly the Polly realized she had been – yet always will stay – exceptional. She did forget it often, but she making it a useful to remember herself in all those moments, they may not concur, but individuals love me. Yeah, she could be cherished and appreciated and it might reminding her of that always. She was feeling proud in being Pollyrma the Fourth, and a comfort in being Dolly the Polly —but more importantly, she realized it felt wonderful to be exactly who she was actually.

2.4 Getting Back on Your Toes

Could you assume what it would be like to start walking at the age of 12? Many of us try to stand if we're so small that we miss how we went it. So Brian was like many of us. He was in the passenger seat of his mom's motor car one moist, cold weather afternoon while another driver slammed into them. Brian shrieked of anxiety at the loudness and hostility of the fatal accident. His mother's car was pressed off the route and onto pavement.

Brian wasn't a whiner. He rode motorcycles professionally and was familiar with crashing and risking injury — but perhaps he just injured. His mother had been harmed as well. This was the scariest thing that's happened to him. He struggled hard to get up and rescue his mother and he was unable to do so He felt powerless and terrified. His brain hurt while he was having aches all along his right hand side.

Luckily, the clinic evaluations did not showed any bone fractures or something severe, and the physician said he might go back to the house. But the aches were not stopping. Brian noticed it growing tougher to walk around. He could not really keep a glass in his hands now without crashing. He had little ability to break the round top on a drinking can, or keep his pen in class. His knees were so fragile he was still tipping over. Moving got more and more difficult, till he could hardly step at all. And that he was afraid to get back into a car. That's not Brian's style. He was a brave kid. He performed boxing training, raced with buddies on his Dirt bike, and rode his motorcycle. His living room bookshelf was filled with medals that he had collected.

Today, he was powerless to do either of such things. He spent time watching television, using X-Box and feeling terrible. His eyes light up as his friends thought about riding a motorcycle. You rode on mountain bike. You favored swampy paths and hops. His friends were thinking about what he was doing when you dropped off his motorcycle in a race. How did he get up on his feet again? What lead to getting out on the wheel and finishing?

Brian should have to start walking properly. You might not know what it felt like before you even started to walk, and for the first occasion you might envisage how it sounds like for just a little child to get up on his feet. It needs to be difficult just to stand up at some point. Those small muscles in the legs are feeble and not yet prepared to stand. You probably took a lot of falls at first, just like that young child, but you were not put off. You ended up getting up to stand on your toes each moment you started falling, perhaps at first with a little wobbly, sometimes trying to take help from an assisting arm or stair railing. Through time you grew much stronger before you could walk through your own feet. Then you started moving one toe next to another, heading forward for the first time. Then you likely had a few slips, but every time you turned up and tried then, each day you got stronger and smarter. Eventually you ran and jumped and skipped and didn't really think about how to start moving the muscles in the body to stroll to a friend's apartment, kick a ball or ride a bicycle.

This is how it was for twelve-year - old Brian. He had to know how to go through this again. Recognizing he once did it assisted him to experience the faith to do that again. It had not been convenient. In reality, there were times when it was grueling job. Luckily Brian wasn't loser. He realized what to do to get back and complete the match on his bike. Without having fallen he started walking again, to ride bikes, and to hit a football. Who would presume you might have to remember at the age of 12 how much you have previously mastered at the age of 12?

2.5 Understanding Perks of Sharing

Once upon a time two states shared same frontier. One nation had been paved with boulders, governed by a queen. Other one, which was governed by a monarch, that would've been all right, but the queen kept looking over the frontier, and anticipated whatever the man had. "We can plant crops of clear land," she went on to say, "and give my citizens."

Then, the king looked over the frontier as well, and needed whatever the woman had. "We might build infrastructure, hospitals and schools, with the rock formations," he stated ". The queen always said her citizens, "since we are trying to feed we have to clear our ground. Toss all the rocks across the frontier. The stone less state people have been going to their emperor and whined. "The people in society of the queen throw rocks at us," they added: ".

"We wouldn't want to build homes, hospitals & schools on stones? "Said the king. 'Come wage war. The citizens of the queen are weak and having no other arms, except the stones. If they continue tossing stones, we'll get all the resources we want to construct our homes.' And the fighting went on till the stone less field was filled of rocks and the stony field was stone less. The citizens of both the King as well as the Queen were content for a time. Citizens of the queen farmed the land on clear soil. The persons of the emperor built houses, hospitals and schools. For a period. The princess soon realized they will have plenty of nutrition but no rocks for constructing new houses, schools, and hospitals. They didn't have rocks to rebuild the old houses. The emperor's citizens then had dozens of building structures on the other side of the divide but fresh produce was limited and they were super hungry.

"We should have a battle to get our pieces back," the queen stated, so another battle was proclaimed. Once again the rocks were thrown over the frontier. Citizens of the king and queen continued engaging, seeking what both had, but nobody was satisfied. Then, a roaming village idiot ended up coming to rest on a mountain close to the border. To see what was going on, he broke out guffawing. "This is crazy," he muttered to himself and invited the royal family together to talk. They were not very cordial at first until they sat up face to face. "That it's all your responsibility," the king stated "."You started this by throwing stones at us."

"No, it's your fault," the queen replied. "You've waged war on others to get the resources." "Hold on, hold on," said only the clown. "It's not going to overcome your major issue if you're frustrated or criticizing one another. One of you've got rocks. One of you've got farms. But you're heading to only want what another does have until you get it. The clown noticed both the king and the queen thinking regarding his statement. The king replied again. "The rocks are yours," he said to the queen. "The farmlands are with us, but the clown is correct. We just want what another has. Perhaps we should trade it. How about food production for you, and exchanging it for the rocks we require. Perhaps my citizens should instruct a few of your citizens how and when to plant. The queen accepted and the clown smiled pleasantly. Because after two nations decided to share all they had and lived peacefully together, the clown sometimes would relax on his slope, observing the citizens coming over the border, exchanging grain and rocks.

2.6 Tackling Tribulations: Children's Story

Ellie and Eddie were dinosaurs. In simple terms, they have always been 2 extremely curious young dinosaurs that enjoyed to discover new gameplay and experience new things. They grew up with a household of dinosaurs in a luscious canyon as there were clean rivers as well as plenty of vegetables and fruits. Life is wonderful.

A day Ellie and Eddie were trying to explore a grotto throughout the highlands that encircled their village. They plunged down deep into the grotto, each motivating another, intrigued to see just how far those who could discover — while unexpectedly externally there had been a bang. Ellie and Eddie began running towards its opening of the grotto to search that their verdant village and community of pterosaurs had vanished. After all course, they still doesn't understand what was happening, but it was going to be thousands of years ever since researchers will indeed reveal that an asteroid must have smacked their village and destroyed out almost everything except ellie and Eddie, which had been concealed beneath the surface within the grotto. Initially, they stayed in the opening to the grotto and glanced out across the valley, completely shocked. They found it weird. After which sorrow settled on each other because they became conscious of their misfortune.

Having a look out across scorched valley, ellie was first to discuss. "This is dreadful! "She stated ". "It's the toughest thing one will ever face. How are we ever going to get over this? "And she felt much sadder about that. Eddie Answered, "Yeah of course, what has actually occurred is awful, but is it not nice that we've been discovering the cave? We'll appreciate we managed to survive. We are so happy. "And she seemed far less depressed at that thought — definitely not much, but maybe perhaps a little less depressed.

"Indeed, but we've missed it all," ellie replied. "Our extended clan, all our mates, all our meals and all our drinks. Our house is ruined to the full. "Could things get worse," Eddie answered. "We do have each other at least. The dust is now starting to settle; we will see the sky again and over the hills there might be another valley that is unseen. We will maybe see how many people have lived outside this gorge. "I wouldn't like any," ellie added. "I have way so much suffering inside myself. Why does this happening to me? My future is in ruin.'

"It will bring change and make it easier," Eddie said. "None of it remains the same now. It was sunny and warm as we went into the tunnel. All looked relaxed and they were doing business. Once we were in there shifted unexpectedly. It's definitely going to improve and again begin having better.

"It will never be," ellie stated. Her thoughts were sounding heavier on her soul and for every phrase she said, her emotions became weirder. "No, it isn't going to be the exact as it was," Eddie decided. "Do not let us lose faith for the possibilities. Maybe we should continue doing stuff to make life easier than it is. "And the sorrow disappeared just a little further as she looked ahead. "Situations couldn't get much worse," ellie stated "."I have missed everything and everyone. What are we going to do? Nothing works right anymore. "She kept saying this stuff again and again in her mind the more she appears to have done, even worst she felt but the less she started to feel like doing anything other than just lounging at the entry of the cave watching the scorched valley and crying a lot.

"Come on," Eddie said, prodding Ellie back at her side. "Nothing we intend to do. We have to keep moving on to find a better life and buddies. "Ellie moving was not really convenient, however as quickly as Eddie was up and walking she surely felt much better. Although both Eddie and ellie have witnessed the very same tragic part, we guess which one you believe would better deal with it. How did Eddie think and what did she do that enabled her dealing with it relatively easy? How else could Ellie change her thinking and the stuff she'd do to make it right?

2.7 Making the right Choice

Kyle was out to the zoo for a class trip. All understood that Kelly had a fantastic memory — especially Kyle himself. He may be captain of a spacecraft flying to the Alpha Jovian glittering galaxy, a million light - years from earth, throughout algebra class. He could be driving his mystical frequency-machine motorcycle into the futures of science. He may lead a Kyle-designed, stress-resistant vessel in English to the Mariana Trench, the lowest location on land, 30,000 feet below. The group was still at the theme park on an elevated platform gazing down into the nature park in Tanzania. But amongst all the creatures Kyle was off. We do not even realize if he actually thought he was still there or if it were his imagining.

Anyway, he might saw himself as the a fantastic adventurer if he would let his imaginations run wild: a silver rind cap on his forehead, big tan leather shoes on his foot, khaki trousers and a coat with side pockets. Unexpectedly a noisy — and extremely close — rumble struck. Kyle had a massive, famished-looking lion eye to eye. Its big, bushy, dark hair covered a face with a wide mouth wide open and broad, pointed teeth in it. As Kyle glanced around a way to flee he could see that the whole group of lions have surrounded him. A roaring river surrounded his only escape path. "What should I do? "Kyle astonished. He would really needed to think fast. So what are his options? He could perhaps sprint but lions could also move faster than he would have. He was able to scale the nearby tree but he recalled the lions still climbed trees in certain parts of Africa. Was that right here? He stared at the river which was roaring. Could sink if he fell in. What would he do? He had just seen a moderately-submerged sheet floating in the water.

He jumped on the wood with one ever-powerful leap, happy to avoid the lions. Then he has felt the squirm of the wood. He felt it all over again. Swimming in the log! This wasn't just that logging. He was cruising a crocodile upon its back. How will he do now? And he noticed a further growl, a further sound, the growl of a waterfall plunging into blankness over a high slope.

Finally Kyle made a choice: sit on the crocodile's rear and be steamrolled across the river, dive to the coast and maybe be swallowed by the alligator, or touch one of those elongated trees. Selecting the tree, he jumped, only winding his fingertips around the bark where he perched over the croc's cracking teeth.

He was standing face to face with a snake trying to carry himself into the tree! Maybe not all snakes are toxic, Kyle recalled, but enough of anyone who isn't ready to eviscerate their mouths and gulp down a teenage child's size or animals. What will he do presently? What choice did he have? He might ascend further but would they sustain his load, while the branches grew slimmer? The snake was smaller than Kyle, and still might rise higher. He may leap but the lions would still have no problem taking a bite of him if he lost a leg. He could see so a vine sticking from a tree. Perhaps he could move towards the next tree like Tarzan, then jump safely to the ground.

He jumped back over to the next tree and pulled the bonnet down. His toes had hardly hit the floor so if he felt he was grabbed from behind by someone else. What should it have been? Is it a bear going to sweep him up and run him to mortality? Was it a cheetah that reached out to grind him in a massive hug? He started to turn in with a park ranger to find itself eye to eye. "Sonny," the park ranger stated, "We'd better move you out of here someone thinks that you could make an odd dietary adjustment." Kyle made a different decision. How dare the guy obstruct a brilliant adventurer from Africa! Should Kyle gain freedom and flee off to the forest experiences, or go to reenter his school party with the keeper? We doubt what he'd decided the said moment.

2.8 Restructuring with Positivity

A kid was going to his home from taking class at school until he noticed the stems of an apple tree sticking out of a big fence. By one of the limbs hung a big, enticing apple. The kid weren't more of a fruits-eater, choosing a candy bar if offered the alternative, however, like they say, the impermissible fruit could be enticing. And seeing apple, the kid needed it. The more he stared at it, the insatiably hungry he started feeling and that the more he would like that apple.

He stepped on toes, trying to stretch as top as he could, although at his highest point elevation he was still unable to approach it. He started to leap. He jumped in the air, arising as top as he could, at the highest point of each climb trying to stretch his arms to pick up the apple. It nevertheless stayed out of grasp. He assumed even more about how he would solve his issue. He assumed maybe he could move up the fence, but as he confronted its towering, flat finish he could try to figure nothing at all to grip — no foot-holds, no hand-holds, hardly anything. Argh.

Not surrendering, he considered, maybe if he had anything to stand on. His backpack will not give sufficient altitude and he really don't want to tear the stuff within it, like his lunch box, pencil sharpener, and Game toy.

Going to look just over, he wished he could perhaps find an old container, a stone, or, luckily, even a ledge, but that was a clean suburb and he'll use hardly anything. He might have done it all that he could dream of doing. He decided to give up not finding any other choices, and kept walking. He started to feel upset and frustrated at first having thought about how starving he might have been from his attempts, how much he really wished the apple, or how fresh and tasty it would've been for him to dig his dentures into his body. The longer he felt this way — the more he was worried of what he might have skipped — the far more depressed and dissatisfied he was.

The kid in our tale, though, was indeed a fairly smart person, even though he did not get what he desired. He began to say to himself, that's not beneficial don't really have an apple and I feel lousy, too. There's just nothing that I'm doing to get the apple — which is unalterable — but we should be able to alter our emotions. If that's the situation what can I do to cheer myself up?

Maybe if I consider about the apple differentially, I could perhaps feel very differently, he added, throwing out many thoughts. The apple just certainly doesn't belong to me and it would have been wrong to take it. Maybe the fruit was also not ready and I could have a bad tummy ache by now, if I had ingested it.

When he started to think about those feelings he immediately felt better. He then said himself softly, "I 'm happy I couldn't touch it." The more he felt, the more he was and the better he felt, the more he wanted to go on having thought the things that left him feeling extremely happy.

2.9 Looking for Suppleness

Once there had been a mouse named Jim Rodent, living in a hole in a wall at the building's side. There had been a tap on the wall above the opening in his house one winter morning when Jim Mouse was enjoying his buttered sandwiches for breakfast. "Could we

Get inside? "A shrill voice called, but a long, slender nose jabbed via the pit that Jim had known as Gary. "Definitely, step in," Jim replied, trying to Sound much more assured than he did feel. He absolutely adored Gary, but he was still very afraid of him and that lemurs, like squirrels and fleshy otters, have loads and loads of bristly feathers, and Gary's quills really seemed to stick up, even at the right moments. Gary had to pinch and wobble into the tiny door-hole of Jim, but because echidnas are accustomed to digging, he eventually squeezed in. And when he did, his pointed, bristly antlers shot up. Sure, Jim would be one of those nice kinds of mice who want to give a huge, big hug to their truly unique buddies to welcome them, but Gary was one individual he stepped aside from. "Can I move up, too? "One other long, slender nasal was told to peek via the door." Yeah," Jim added. Emily, a neighbor of Gary, also walked in the door, her itchy welts sticking up like Gary's. Their feathers were shaking, Jim thought. "What an error? "Jim kept asking. "It's just so dark," Gary said. "The night was cold and it was also freezing cold on the mountain side in the Rocky Mountains at which we stayed. So we started rolling up into a ball and fell down the mountain as quickly as we could see if we just arrive and warm up in your comfortable tiny home. Jim could see Gary sliding down a hill with Emily You recognize, if lemurs are in risk they have2 ways to make their way out of distress.

Firstly, if they are attacked by any species, they will hold up their fangs so that no one else get near them and harm them. Maybe a little because when kids get upset, it gives out a warning that simply says, "Step off or otherwise. "If they're frightened the second thing lemurs do seems super hilarious to anyone viewing. They fold like a puck, so that they slide down to just get away from trouble if they're just next to a very little ridge or slope. That's how they landed at Jim's residence —like a few beach balls heading down from highlands. Jim figured it had to be a nice way to get there from one location to the next. "And in our hiding place, "Gary said, "Was ice cold. "Emily stated: "When I was trying to get near to him, his prickles were caught. If we could just snuggle close, we'd actually keep one another cozy throughout the winter.

"So, we figured that we should descend and see you," Gary added. "Your house is cozy and warm in the tiny hole at the corner of the building and you're not just a dear person. We had thought you could tell us how to fix our issue.

It was already early today, so Jim had to consider a while until answering, so he gave some buttered baked beans for breakfast to Gary so Emily. They wouldn't seem as glad of buttered sandwiches as Jim thought, and they refused, stating they should go out smelling for their own nutrition as the day was getting a little colder. They declined his offer of a nice cup of cocoa, though. "the very first thing that appears to me," Jim explained, "is that your fibers have the true purpose of helping to shield you from larger predators that could harm you and hold you on. This is good if a wild animal or a flying eagle starts to believe that you may be giving them an enticing meal. If you'd like to live, it's necessary to always have them, but since when are you under real threat like this? "He was wondering. Gary and Emily looked to each other and laughed, "Actually, not so much," Gary added. "But while it's important to make your whiskers often stick up," Jim continued, "there are a lot of the time you may not need them. I'm maybe a little mouse and realize there's just no way can I harm you, but your fibers stick out like spears stuck floppy-end-out of a goal. As a consequence, I'm far further apart from you than I'd would like. And then I'd love to offer you an embrace. "Although it can be beneficial to be stubbly occasionally and in certain cases," he added, "it isn't beneficial to be so testy all the same in every position. Maybe you could merely try to let your guard down for a while and then take it easy even these fibers while you're secure in my residence. Nothing or anyone here can harm you.' Emily and Gary attempted. We attempted tough. They still tried desperately, but the hairs had sticked up completely that it was just what they wanted to do. "I have no idea what to do about it," Gary stated. "It sounds like that's exactly how I always did. "For a second shut your eyes," Jim said, "and imagine there's a huge lion coming to consume you."" But in that region, that there were no lions," Gary insisted. "Keep your eyes closed just there, and dream of a wild, starving-looking beast, moving slowly towards you." When Gary and Emily shut their eyes, their still hanging-up hairs got much up righter. "Fine "Jim said. "So dream of a quiet spot or a peaceful moment, perhaps back inside your own mound on an fun afternoon after you've just had a great meal and can dream about resting or enjoying that little lunch break. "When Gary and Emily first saw secure place, they started lowering their fangs only a bit, not much at all, just a little. "Fine "Jim added. "Now carry on working" Jim looked like a doctor treating them a drug for some medication. "Practicing this every day as soon as you wake up or every sleep when you go to rest, could help. Start talking in scenarios where you need to keep your whiskers up, and also about calm moments, safe ways to let them drop. Avoid telling oneself why you ought to bring them around, or buddies like me."

A short time later, as he regularly did, while Jim was enjoying his buttered sandwiches for brunch, a tap arrived on the wall next to his main entrance. A long, slender muzzle lodged in the door, and whispered, "Should we get in? "And Gary and Emily crouched Incas their fangs lied peacefully across their skins, Jim offered them a large embrace to each beyond fear of spiking.

And they got him embraced again. "The air has been freezing," Jim said, "but since you last went, you're not cowering as often as you did."

"No "Emily responded. "Now we're not as seethe towards one another we can snuggle together10 times more and hold one another cozy through the chilly days. It's a lot better.' "Yes "Gary decided. "We think we 'd like to tell you just because you helped show us that there may be moments when it's okay to be thorny and moments when it's good not just to be,. "Jim thought what they'd do when he led Gary and Emily back up the mountain into the highland. They showed Jim how to curl up into a ball with their fibers off, and the 3 of friends started going down the icy mountain side, flailing into the thick piles of snow at the base, grinning maniacally.

2.10 Pleasure Boosts

Sandy's real identity was Philip but for as far as he can to recall, people had nicknamed him Sandy. It came as a shock when he found that Phillip was his real identity. It was hard to imagine how "Sandy" could've been extracted from "Phillip. "The two words seemed, and appeared so distinct when they were written. He made a point of saying he was named Sandy, when he so deeply enjoyed the sandy beach. Going to think that looked and felt as if he was intended to be together with the beach, that they did belong around each other. This was sandy beach because he was Sandy. The parents drove from their residence in the town to the house on the beach at the beginning of the summer holiday, generally having arrived late in the evening. All had settled in by time the car was unloaded, and dinner was served, it was time to sleep. Sandy probably wouldn't mind getting laid to rest since he couldn't wait until sooner the next morning to wake up. He couldn't possibly run down to the beach, feeling the fine sand beneath his feet. He could not really take long to get down to the ground and feel the smooth pixilated sand gobbling up his hands. He understood how to tap it in a sandy design, how to build stiffer with every touch, how to smoot his palms down each side and form his layout. Often it was a tower, maybe a dragon could've been built, and often a sandman would be created. Waterlogged, colder and lighter when dry, the sand felt hard, thick and dry. He was able to envision anything he liked, and create it.

He enjoyed the sunny solar wind soothing comfort on his skin, yet he was mature enough to realize, without ever being advised, to hide, to put on a cape, and to sunscreen so that the light did not destroy his skin an unpleasant red. Gosh, what a sensation he was running down to the beach and jumping into the cool, tangy water! He would lay on his back and float carelessly, as if he were being guided by some caring side. Hovering in the water felt very much safer and kinder than since he had done it at the pool where he was going to swim lessons with his family. The freezing cold wind has started to turn his skin squirrel-bumpy at the end of the day. He loved all the ambient noise she'd never listened at residence. Falling asleep in the house on the beach the very first night really was exceptional. Drifting off to the waves crashing spinning the shoreline was so amazing, particularly since you never quite knew in what frame of mind they could be in. They'd be smashing, heavy, and intense occasionally, while at other moments they'd be delicate and pleasant — a quiet, shifting sound around the sand They were normal at moments, ripple after ripple, and they'd be noisy and puzzled at some. Sandy stayed in bed having a good match of his breath on the tides. It was always the last element he recalled before listening to the amusing yapping and wrangling noises of the seagulls struggling for a leftover food patch in the dawn.

He'd slide down his passenger window as they headed to the house on the beach, hoping for that first salty whiff of the water. Sometimes, before reaching the brushy rock formations, he would sense it in the air and get their first sight of the sea. Up early in the morning Sandy was discovering what was washing up at the beach by the high tide. He could perhaps find pellets of solar-bleached cuttlefish, a brightly colored jellyfish, or prickly pieces of driftwood coated in strange plankton. One holiday, he noticed the tall, small, greenish shell behind a turtle. Polished particles, scuttling crabs and small, flitting trout stood in the large, deep rocky shores. He thought that a giggly snake was a swirling silver substance left behind by ocean. He might find tiny bits of shrimp in brown clumps, smarmy shrimp that he might pop through his fingertips. Sandy felt more at home on the shoreline sands, and we guess it's why he assumed his initials truly started from that place.

2.11 Jeff and his Anger

Jeff was a quite good guy .He absolutely loved his family members, and they actually liked him mainly. We assume, "mainly" because Jeff might get really mad occasionally. He may cry out and yell at others if stuff can't go quite his manner. He would just try to smash the gates, drag other children around instead toss stuff that happened to be near to him. His mother and father had always said statements like, "You really should try and control that anger, small boy, and you'll get into massive trouble someday." Lately Jeff found that a few of his fellow students seemed to ignore him far more. And more upset he was, therefore less moments they wish to spend with him. This made Jeff nervous. He had a preference for his colleagues. He won't want to lose kids but wasn't aware on what to do with it. He was always this manner. Try as he could, problems would occasionally stack up like a mountain before it exploded. Jeff started to feel this was out of his grasp. What is it he might do?

His father came home from the supermarket one weekend saying ", "Jeff, I have a gift for you." He dragged a brand-new mallet and pack of big, sparkly nails out of the grocery bag. He had an aged can of cooked-bean and nudged the nails in the empty bucket. Giving Jeff the latest mallet and can of screws, he said, "Whenever you get mad, go out and bang a nail into the fence post running down the building's side. "Initially, Jeff had felt that his elderly man may have to go weird or some kind of. He could have been under excessive work pressure but Jeff gave a grimace. He had done all the rest, then why not do as his dad had just said?

Each time he turned mad at residence he ended up going to the side railing and pounded a nail. When he was upset at school he would recall how many occasions he had lost his cool and as soon as he's done he would go hammering in the fence the right figure of nails. Jeff eventually realized the job of banging the nails in getting really boring. He can't stand having to keep a record of all the moments he was upset and afterwards get out in the garden, grab the nails and crowbar, stroll over to the railing and pound in an another few nails, notably if it was rainy and cold. Jeff realized unexpectedly he was becoming less and less frustrated.

In reality, it was easier to manage his aggression than recall the times that he didn't have, then go and pound a further nail in the railing. He happily came out and told his father after a week of not facing up against the fence, except on a particular instance. "Fine" his father stated.

"I am very glad to hear that. I would like you to go out and eliminate a few of those nails you pummeled in the railing each day without losing your cool. The weeks pass by and the nails pulled a few at a moment however Jeff found that they had been causing openings everywhere in the process of extracting them. The timber skipped around several holes, locking them up a bit while others remained the wood dowel's full thickness. Jeff was preoccupied with the holes that existed long after he replaced the nails. When he tried to tell his father, his father replied, "What occurs if we get enraged is a little like this way. Rage can damage and it means leaving a laceration or bruise that somehow individuals understand hard after the rage has managed to pass.

During coming days Jeff was thinking about the statements of his father. He didn't get the impression he managed to leave holes inside the railing. He saw the bruises that resulted through his actions each time he went by it. He asked his father for some plasticine the next Friday and covered all the cracks in the railing but he was still able to see where they'd been. Jeff decided to undo what he had done, so, that weekend, he requested his father if he may spray the railing. "What color do you want to use? "His father inquired. Jeff handsome suggestions. He might paint the barricade all in one color, paint a specific hue for each pole, or do a mosaic all over the railing. Maybe he'd have a ledge-painting session that would invite his buddies over to do some artwork. He found there were a lot of things that he'd do which might modify what he might have done to the railing. The latter, Jeff figured, is much more entertaining than banging down nails.

2.12 How to Differentiate

When you're rising up it 'shard to understand the expectations of you. Mother says, "Do the utensils, "and father says, "Do you school work." father says, " Come here, "and mother says , "do that." we are sure you understand what we are saying. What are you doing? What's really alright and which is not? How do you realize? That's the quandary Charlie was in. His mother and father had a few acquaintances going to visit while out of town. These acquaintances would also have two kids: George, who's a little older than Charlie, and Brandon, who's a little youthful. Whereas the two sides of the family sat chatting over espresso after meal, the boys vanished into Charlie's bedroom and were shortly coarse-housing and have pillow battles with one another. The mother and father had a giggle about it, making comments about how "Boys would be boys.

Afterward, going to visit the community park, the family sat and talked whereas the kids stayed back, even now bumpy-housing. Once Brandon, the younger son, got trashed to the floor and popped up weeping, Charlie got a lesson from his father — probably since he looked sillier than George did. "Hold on," stated "Brandon's mom, attempt to soothe the issue a bit. "They were all doing what they 'redoing home early with the cushions before."" Yes, "stated "Charlie's dad, "but they'll have to understand to discern the difference among when it's alright to fool around and then when it's not. They have to understand when it 'safe and then when it violent and dangerous. Brandon might just have banged his head-on one of stones by the road. Charlie felt terrible. He have not wanted to hurt Brandon. They had both been trying to fool together like at school, as Brandon's mom said. Or how can you know when one moment is good but when others is not? Charlie's dad's rage was an illustration. Charlie was already being advised not to be upset, but he saw his father come home furious from work from time to time and he certainly saw his father get mad at the referee when they headed to the sporting event on Sundays.

In addition, often his father might stand up and yell and hard that Brandon often felt ashamed to be around him. And he never saw his father get mad around Mother, and never mad with him. And Charlie thought, when has it been okay but when is it not nice?

"You must always reveal the truth, "kept insisting both his mommy and daddy. Yet he had discovered that if he said the truth he might get into danger. However, he had learned his mother tell friends how she had other intentions when the friend invited her out. And Charlie realized she didn't have any other plans, after all. He'd even seen Father call his manager one morning and say he had a very terrible headache but wouldn't be working that same day, when Charlie knew he didn't have a pain but decided to go out with Mother. At the end of the trip, Charlie's parents and the companions paused at the restaurant in the park for a cocktail. The restaurant had a little shelter with some teenage white kangaroos who were playing. They adjusted on their powerful tails, started punching one another with their legs, and slashed out with their lengthy back legs. An audience had stopped to watch in obsession. People had taken photos.

It's alright for us kids to ragged-house in my place, thought Charlie, just not have this in the field. It's alright for the kangaroos to combat and box in the park, but I think Mother will go crazy if they tried it in my house. No doubt it's overwhelming. How else could Charlie come to learn what has been okay or what wasn't when he got information like that? He definitely have not tried to scare Brandon and, thankfully, he also don't; and yet we suppose he was a little cleverer from the knowledge even though he began wondering: if he would haven't did it wrong the whole time, how would he do it better next time?

In his head, Charlie start to question oneself some queries. Is it secure for someone like me to do just what I'm doing? Is it likely to injure me or somebody else? If we've played, how could we have enjoyment and do it securely? One aspect might be good with one set of situations or for one crowd of mates but not for others. How do I evaluate that? Did wonder Charlie. Of instance, things still happen that we may not wish to occur at times, so there will not be any definite responses to those issues, so by raising them Charlie put itself in a great place to recognize in the future what has been good or what wasn't.

Magic Dreams Bedtime Stories

A Collection of Short Tales For your Kids to Help Them Fall Asleep Easily and Felling calm

By Anna Smith

Chapter 1: Meditation Stories for Kids

If from a young age we could channel the mindfulness meditation, what will the future look like? Here's why we need our children to follow a daily meditation method, and how in the long term, instead of stressful activities such as incarceration, going by meditation at the present time creates greater good for our children (and us). Do you reap the perks of meditation at present, and wish you started at earlier age, say, as a child? Are you a kid or teenager who is excessively overwhelmed by the today's stressful expectations of modern-day society?

Does your kid have difficulty concentrating on his / her homework? I have trouble with self-esteem? We've all been there, as babies. And as caregivers, relatives, or instructors, by actually bringing them into mediation, we will fix specific issues that children face. Have you ever observed a kid eating their food? They scrutinize it carefully until they take a bite of it — they sniff it, cut it out, scratch it with their teeth, eat it and spit it out.

Naturally, children practice mindfulness — a core component of meditation — as they have fewer mental blocks, perceptions, and pre-determined values that allow them to achieve a pure state of conscience. On the other hand, as adults we actually think that meditation or awareness requires practice and effort, because we need to deliberately rid ourselves of preconceived ideas, fears and beliefs that restrict our natural sense of consciousness. It might sound strange to think of kids as relaxed, non-judgmental, and attentive, but in the end, kids can gain consciousness and thereby learn meditation more quickly than adults do. So it's fair to say that integrating relaxation into a child's academic experience is better than we thought and with promising outcomes, classrooms across the U.S. have been introducing relaxation to their curriculum.

A Baltimore school recently replaced detention (a conventional way of punishing misbehaving children by having them sit in silence for 1 hour or more in a classroom) with a more progressive form of behavioral evaluation: meditation. Instead of the tedious and, in most situations, the unhelpful cycle of incarceration, educating children to reflect on their breath and to be in the current moment can in the long run gain greater benefit. Even better, teaching children outside detention by implementing it regularly as part of school programs or at home can help children avoid the very reasons that landed them in detention in the first place. Although work into how meditation influences and helps children isn't as rigorous and comprehensive as it is for adults, it sure starts to take off. Below are some of the benefits that research tells us can offer children to mediate and to be mindful.

1.1. Benefits of Meditation

The child's subconscious continually investigates, asks, explores and develops suppositions.

Meditation helps children settle in on this process and help them learn to regulate their emotions and achieve cognitive growth.

While meditation importance and benefits to adults, such as less stress and better decision-making skills, this practice gives children a different set of benefits. Let's look at the top five benefits of children's meditation, and why you should introduce children as soon as possible to a simple daily practice of meditation.

1. Meditation Improves attention

Noticed how much more children in our young people are drawn to gadgets, social media, and technology than we ever were? Modern demands are increasingly challenging us to think and respond faster than ever before-and children are no exception. Constant pressure during the waking hours of children — from the internet, computer games, social media, school tasks — demands that they multitask and switch from thought to thought.

While multitasking and simultaneously juggling many different physical, mental, emotional, and social tasks or activities can sometimes be a good thing:

You want your child to turn its focus to one thing at a time absolutely.

You want your child to be in a position to solve difficult problems and see projects to completion. You want that your child has the ability to concentrate. A study by Italian neuroscientist Giuseppe Pagnoni found that meditation not only changes brain patterns but also increases mental focus which can improve cognitive function.

In the study, brain scans indicate that non-meditators had higher activity in their ventral posteromedial cortex as compared to those who meditate, the region of the brain associated with spontaneous thoughts and mind-walking.

So when your child needs a little boost of concentration and clarification next time, look no further than a quick meditation to more good understanding with laser emphasis.

2. Meditation fosters self-confidence and self-love

Most of us as children, at one time, felt like we were not "good enough." Childhood can be tough, especially during puberty, and in many cases weakening our self-esteem and trust. Of course, most of our current insecurities may have originated in childhood: A state of embarrassment that haunted you. Not being the school "cool boy." Not having a car like "this." Being bullied — any situation of childhood that impressed trauma, or any negative belief about yourself. Happily, meditation gives access to a greater sense of inner stability and security. Meditation slows down the movement of the mind (self-talking and obsessive thinking) to achieve calm, inner harmony, self-love and happiness as a way of quieting the mind. When you learn to focus on the moment, it transforms your fears, self-doubt and insecurities.

3. For peak performance, meditation relieves tension

Stress can start affecting children at a very young age, and stressful situations almost immediately affect health and wellbeing. Academic expectations, rivalry, and constantly trying to "get it right" take a massive toll on children's ability to relax. Bluntly put, excessive stress hinders peak performance. Like adults, meditation can help kids deal with tension and anxiety by being aware of current circumstances and talking about them simply and rationally. The body follows when the mental is calm. When the mind is tension-free it should work at its best.

Because meditation is known to help children focus their energies and lessen tensions, evidence shows that it can assist them perform better in school. Meditation, in addition, may have a significant impact not just on academics but also on physical, artistic and public performance.

A research by the University of California, Los Angeles, showed that second and third graders who performed "mindful" meditation methods for eight weeks for 30 minutes twice a week had changed behavior and scored better on recall, concentration, and awareness measures than the non-meditators.

More and more schools incorporate meditation into their learning programs and it is only a matter of time that meditation becomes a standard for academic initiatives.

4. Meditation claims to support positive emotional growth

Kids have to face even more "fears" in our fast-paced lifestyle than ever before.

Doubts of not being accepted, fears of changing too much, fears of losing loved ones or simply fears of not being "enough."

Without too much distress, we want children to be able to navigate through phases of insecurity, frustration and impatience.

Yet chronic fear-based tension can be detrimental on the mental growth of a child and have long-term consequences.

Fortunately, mindfulness allows children to access their natural rhythm of self-awareness and awareness — two key components of self-reassuring, problem-solving, patience, and fear-fighting.

5. Meditation increases mindfulness and communication

Meditation is commonly known to increase compassion — empathy and compassion stem directly from the state of mind awareness, a distinct outcome of meditation on mindfulness. But there is now concrete, empirical proof of how meditation on mindfulness enhances empathy, sensitivity, and communication for both adults and children. Researchers observed in a study at Northeastern University that "meditation has made people able to behave virtuously — to help someone who is hurting — even in the face of a tradition not to do so."

Researchers aren't sure exactly why mindfulness enhances empathy and communication, but there are 2 potential explanations. Secondly, therapy increases the attention-span of kids and their capacity to concentrate on different issues in their world. Second, mindfulness creates neural connections that enable children to see human suffering interconnected irrespective of their relationships. Regular loving-kindness or careful mindfulness builds a multi-level connection between self-love, compassion, and human or environment. By teaching children meditation, you will help them become conscious of this normal condition and thus help them conquer any disruptive, bad feelings.

1.2. Two Rats

Two rats had once been there and were good friends. Another lived in a town and the other lived in a forest. Each of them shared news of their well-being with other rats in the city and village who moved between the two locations. Once the city rat decided to speak with a relative of his village. He conveyed the message by several village rats. The guest at the village was very enthusiastic about meeting his parents. Preparations were made to welcome him. He went to the village border to receive his friend, wearing a traditional dress such as dhoti, kurta, and cap, with a garland in his hand. His friend from town, however, was wearing a suit, boots and a neck tie. They kissed and traded salutations. The village rat greeted him and said, "Here we have fresh and unpolluted air, the environment in the town is unclean." They have chattered a lot and shared opinions on different subjects. They sat down, then, to eat. The rat in the village served him fruit and boiled grains of wheat.

After eating, they went outside the village for a stroll. The plains were turning lush and the jungle's natural beauty had its own appeal. "Does the city have such lovely scenes?" asked the village rat, "The city rat asked nothing but welcomed the village rat to come to the city at least once to see the city's nice existence. The village rat said one day he will probably be coming to the area.

The town rat said, "Why don't you go with me now?" The village rat replied, "Okay, I'll consider your proposal."

They came back when the night fell, and slept on the soft grass. Next day the village rat served fresh fruits and cereals to his friend for breakfast. The city rat was irritated and told the village rat, "Let's go to town right now. Give me an opportunity to serve you."

The village rat accepted the proposal, and was prepared for the city trip. The rat in the town stayed in a big house. The village rat was surprised to see at night, the dining table full of various types of dishes. Before the village rat saw no such variety of foods. The village rat was told to eat the meal by the town rat. Then, he began eating. The village rat liked the paneer, and quickly finished the plate. At this moment they heard a cat's voice. The city rat said, "Rapidly hide under the almirah, or the cat will destroy us." Everyone ran to the almirah, and hid under it. For some time, they all came out as the cat went inside. The village rat was still shivering. The city rat started eating the dishes again and also advised his friend, "Do not be afraid. It's a part of city life." The village rat gathered courage and went back to the dining table. This time he finished his chosen cake easily. A boy came over there with a puppy at this juncture. The village rat, fearing the dog, asked his friend, "Who's this fellow?" The city rat said, "He's Jimmi, the master's son of this house, and the dog is his pet. Be quick, and hide yourself there." After they left, both rats came out. The rodent in the village was scared. He said, "Mate, I think I will go back now. I 'm grateful to you for the great food, but there are also risks to it. Thanks again." On reaching, he lifted a sigh of relief and said, "Oh, life is precious and wisdom above all."

1.3. The foolish intimation

A hawk lived on a hill-top a good while ago. There was a banyan tree at the foot of the hill, on which a crow used to perch each day. The crow was extremely foolish. Everybody will copy him. In pursuit of food the hawk on the hill will fly down every day. For long hours, the crow watched the hawk circle in the air, and swooped down when he saw his prey. The hawk bestowed with eyes capable of seeing huge distances would spot his prey from the top of the hill and then fly down to pounce on the prey. The crow stared at the hawk thinking, "Hunh! If that can be achieved by the hawk, then I too can. What is he thinking? I'll show the hawk one day that I can do the same. Several days later, as the hawk circled in the air, the crow made the decision to do the same. Unexpectedly, a baby rabbit came out of the bushes. It was seen by the hawk, and the crow saw the rabbit too. The hawk swooped before the crow could react, caught hold of the rabbit between his high pointed heels and flew away. "Swoosh!" was heard all the crow as the hawk and his prey vanished into the sky. "Mummy! That's no great talent, "the crow, furiously said. Next instant he noticed a big fat mouse coming out of a hole. The crow swooped down without wasting time. He tried to catch the mouse in his claws, like the hawk. Yet the mouse saw the crow, and jumped backwards, crushing the crow into the wall. "Eeeaaa!" the crow screamed in agony. The hawk just then came and flew off. "Hopefully, now you know that hunting isn't easy and that's not easy to imitate either," the hawk said, and flew away. Thereafter, no one in his life was imitated by the crow. He lived happily with the capacities given by God.

1.4. Maurya's magical monsoon morning

Maurya woke up one Saturday morning, when the sun shone in through his eyes. Perched curtains. He was thrilled, for he loved. Playing sunny tennis with daddy

However, as he opened the curtains, it shocked him to see it. Heavily rained, and the sun was shining brightly shone in the gloomy grey clouds. How did it turn out? He wished to know. He ran away in his pyjamas from the house. He

Placed on a high level 21st floor building, but he'd been too excited to wait. That, until it broke open, and the pretty red seeds poured out. Maurya took a handful of the seeds and placed them in his mouth. They tasted good but he felt very odd as he chomped on the seeds. His insides started wiggling and squirming. Maurya was scared and tried to spit the seeds out, but found out

That he couldn't, and then he noticed that his mouth became a beak, A BIG YELLOW BEAK. Now Maurya was really scared. What was it? Will he happen to? Is its poisonous seeds? He looked around at his hands and he found that they had turned feathery and then he saw claws poking out of his bedroom slippers. He had completely transformed himself into a giant black cuckoo bird before he could do anything about it and his pyjamas lay ripped to shreds on the ground. Maurya joyfully ran around the lawn clapping. Unexpectedly he saw something weird. Right in the middle of the lawn was a tree laden with blood red pomegranates. Maurya was sure the pomegranates and tree hadn't been there the day before or ever before. Where were they from? What happened? Curiously exploding, Maurya plucked a grenade. That felt pretty real. He was getting a sudden urge to taste it. But he was unable to open it with his bare fists. So he discovered a strong rock and banged the grenade with it, until it broke open and the beautiful red seeds spill out. Maurya started yelling in panic, but only a throaty "Koo" he could hear. Terrified, Maurya started to wave his arms and run about, but obviously his limbs were no longer free. They had wings! So he found himself in the air soaring in. I will float, he said, stunned. He was in fact so surprised he halted flapping and fell back down, plop. I can fly, thought I can fly Maurya, elated. I always wanted to fly and I can now. So Maurya, forgetting all of his worries, spread his giant wings and took to heaven. He entered the 46th floor where Gamala was a guest of his. He was moving and perching on her glass, and staring through it. Gamala was quickly asleep. Maurya assumed, lazy girl, and yelled her name out. But all that happened to come out was "Koo" a loud screechy Gamala was shocked from her slumber and stared at her window at the giant black bird. Ashamed, she started to throw her toys at her. Maurya managed just about to avoid a red poster colored glass bottle.

Fearing that Gamala would kill him, he soared into the sky higher and wanted to explore the city from the top. The rain fell, and the sunset faded. But it looks like it's made of Legos from up there, Mumbai. Small train cars with long gray lines buttoned up and down. Maurya approached a section of the highway where the building of the metro had just begun. Suddenly four lanes needed to converge to one, causing a massive traffic jam. Maurya remembered that his school bus had been stuck 10 minutes per day at this very location. But now he just must fly over the mess. Delighted he began singing and melodious koos filled the room. Maurya flew merrily over billboards and buildings. All of a sudden he heard the most terrifying sound. At great speed, a huge scary object headed toward him. My favourite! It's a ship, just in time, Maurya realized and veered away. That was a close call, thought Maurya shaking, and decided to stay clear of the airport and look out for the jets. The storm had stopped quite fully. Maurya opted to fly west. He was able to see the open sea from above. He crossed the beach of Juhu, and flew over the waves. But once everything he could see was water, he was terrified. He had never known how vast the sea really was. Maurya sought the sun so that he could fly away from it, back east. Once he could see the shoreline again he was relieved. He had been sick of all this traveling, and he just wanted to relax, but he couldn't stop until he reached the water. He felt thirsty when he reached Juhu beach, and longed for some coconut water. But his beak wasn't successful at pecking through coconut's stiff outer shell. Maurya decided to go south. He remembered that he was sick of being a bird when he flew back but what could he do about it? Maybe his mum will ask. Still, she will remember him? Maurya started crying out thinking he'd be a bird forever. Just then he noticed the building in front of him and landed on the lawn. He had thought it would bring him back to normal eating a few more pomegranate seeds. But the seeds of the pomegranate had disappeared and the tree and fruits had disappeared. They'd vanished like they never were. Maurya walked weeping about. He went to the play area for kids which was his favorite part of the grounds of society. He'd noticed something perched on the slide. The lawn was bone dry and so was the park, with the exception of a small puddle, although it had rained heavily just a short time before. The puddle soon dried too. The odd day had started with the sun shining brilliantly despite the heavy fog, Maurya recalled. He recalled the rainbow that was unnaturally white. Could the rain have been beautiful, he thought. It offered him an idea. In the last few sips of the puddle, he swooped down and drank just like it was drying away. He smiled with a relief as he saw himself transformed into a little boy again. The feathers had gone and he was once again clothed in his pyjamas. Instead of a beak he touched his face and felt soft lips. Mum had coffee and breakfast on the table when he arrived home. Waffles had been his first meal at the weekend. 'You bad boy Maurya. Where were you from? "You know you're not supposed to go out until after breakfast," he shouted. "But mom, it was raining and there was a beautiful rainbow ..." Maurya began. "Oh, enough with the Maurya's lies! Can't you see that the sun shines and there isn't a drop of water in the sky anywhere or a single cloud? "Mom seemed mad, but Maurya secretly ate his waffles. Gamala came to their play date after breakfast." Aunty I saw a giant cuckoo bird today, as big as a puppy, and scared it away with my toys. "She recalled, happily. Maurya says it was raining and you say you have seen a dog-sized cuckoo." "But when the giant cuckoo came to my window, aunty, it was raining. Gamala insisted." Maurya, you should have seen it. It was terrific. I think even bigger than you. "Maurya chuckled and decided to keep his magical epic adventure to himself. Maybe he'd have another soon. Meanwhile today was the ideal sunny day for some tennis with Papa and Gamala.

Chapter 2: Moral stories for learning and better sleep

2.1. The Sad Peacock

There was once a stunning peacock who was dancing on a rainy day. Though he was busy in appreciating his plumage, his ugly voice recalled him of his own weaknesses. He was nearly in tears and the happiness driven out of him. Suddenly nearby, he got to hear a nightingale singing.

Hearing the beautiful sound of the nightingale, his own weaknesses were quite clear once more. He began to wonder why he'd been so jinxed. Juno, who was leader of Gods, arrived at the time and addressed the peacock.

Juno asked the peacock "Why are you upset?

The peacock started complaining about his harsh voice and that he was depressed about it. "This nightingale has a very lovely voice. Why don't I?"

Juno clarified after hearing to the peacock, "every living thing is different in its own way. They are prepared in a way which serves the purpose of the greater. Yeah of course, the nightingale is blessed with a lovely voice, at the same time you too are blessed with a gorgeous and shinning plumage! The logic is to accept, and make the most out of what you have.

The peacock realized how stupid he was to compare himself with others and even to neglecting his own blessings. He learned that day, that in certain way or other, everybody is special.

Moral of the Story

The first step toward happiness is self-acceptation. Make the best of whatever we have, and not being disappointed with what we don't.

2.2. A Tortoise and the Hare

The hare claimed one good day, and came with an idea of having a race with the tortoise. Tortoise accepted, and the contest started.

The hare, as he was an outstanding runner, succeeded to have a nice lead over the tortoise. But that was the hare's ego that he not just moved ahead of the tortoise, but planned to take a nap for some time, before reaching to the finished line. He was sure he would win safely, even though he had been asleep for a little time.

In comparison, the turtle was much slower than the hare. Though, he kept on moving to complete the race, without taking any shortcuts. The turtle tried to reach to the finish line soon as the hare waked up! However, he was a much slow racer than the hare, he won the contest, and he didn't slap his victory on the face of the hare even once.

Moral of the Story

As far as you are persistent and committed, regardless of what your pace is, you will still succeed. Pride, like laziness, is your opponent.

2.3. The Two Gardeners

Once upon a time, there lived two neighbors in their separate gardens, who used to cultivate the similar plants. One neighbor was foolish and treated her plants with great care. The other neighbor did what was needed but decided to leave the plant leaves to grow alone as they satisfied.

A major storm arose one evening, along with heavy rain. The hurricane destroyed several trees.

She found out the plants had been uprooted and destroyed the following morning, when the rude neighbor got up. While when the peaceful neighbor woke up and found her plants already deeply planted in the dirt, having weathered the hurricane.

The happy neighbor's plant had learned to do stuffs alone. So, it had done a bit of its work, gained deep roots, and has made a space in the soil for itself. And also, in the wind, it had stood stable. The fussy girl, though, used to do much for the plant, and therefore did not teach the plant how to support itself.

Moral of The Story

You have to let go sooner or later, to become independent. Nothing can work on its own until you avoid any fussing.

2.4. The Lioness and The Mouse

As we know, the lioness is aggressive, prideful, and appears to look down on smaller creatures. One such lioness once skirting in the forest as her paw was pricked by a thorn. The lioness, being proud, thought, not to call for help. And she wandered around the forest, growing weaker and wounded.

She chanced on a friendly mouse one day. The lioness had been in much pain. Though very terrified, the mouse was brave enough to give help. After a lot of suffering, the little mouse managed to get the thorn out of the paw of the lioness and released her from harm.

Since the lioness was so huge and strong, and the mouse was too small and sweet, it was the gentle act of the mouse which saved the life of the lioness.

Moral of The Story

This tale is never growing older and gives children a great lesson to live with them and aid them flourish.

Stay humble and please remember that size does not guarantee strength or worth.

2.5. Three Fishes

In a pond there were 3 fish. They were good friends and did nearly everything together.

One fine day, the fisherman crossed the pool and enjoyed seeing the birds. He decided to throw a net to trap them.

A separate lake was formed by the cleverest of fishes. The other one declined whereas one of the fish accepted, claiming the pond was his home place and he won't leave it. The third fish said there was never a danger in the pool. "I don't see the reason why this pond should be left. It's cowardly, I believe.

The first two fishes did not convince their mate, so they agreed to separate themselves. The following day, the first two fishes escaped when the fishermen threw their net. The third one was captured, though. He was unable of identifying and dealing with the issue and compensating the price of ignoring the danger.

Moral of The Story

If you have a problem, it's worth being smart. Remember that any problem is unique, and has a unique solution. This tale again tells you how to be smart when dealing with a problem and never forget to help others.

2.6 The Lion and the Mouse

Once in the jungle, a lion was asleep when a mouse began jumping up and down on his body just for enjoyment. This disturbed the sleep of the lion, and he woke up quite angrily. He was about to kill the mouse, when the mouse politely begged the lion to set him free. "I promise you, one day if you save me, I will be of great help to you." The lion laughed at the confidence of the mouse, and let him go.

A few hunters came to the forest one day, and brought the lion with them. They bound him up to a branch. The lion struggled to get out, and began whimpering. The mouse soon walked past and noticed that the lion was in trouble. He raced swiftly and gnawed on the ropes to release the lion. Both ran out of the jungle.

Moral of the Story

A little act of kindness can be going a long way.

2.7. The Lonely Princess

The Empire of Glora was the home for Princess Isabella, a young friendly lady adored by the entire kingdom. Young lady had two older sisters, Juliette and Rose, but she was not like both of them. Rose was pretty sweet so Juliette didn't match her. Nevertheless, to Isabella they both were cruel since they were regarded as conventionally attractive. For her simple look and simplicity, they teased Isabella, and often made fun of that girl for playing with her stuff. They pushed her to dress up extra but Isabella paid little attention to her sisters and kept playing with her dolls. She loved her toys as her names were never called, but she often felt lonely. Her father, King Paul, was disturbed at his youngest child's sorrow, and though he wanted to spend his spare time with her, because of his royal duties he was sometimes called away for longer periods.

The Prince, Geoffrey, of the Kingdom of Meadow-Hill, reached the Kingdom of Glora on a bright summer morning, seeking out a bride. He'd been one year younger than Juliet, a year elder than Rose, and 2 years elder than Isabella. All of the sisters were keen on meeting the beautiful prince. Geoffrey Prince talked to Juliette for the very first time, praising her lovely dresses. Pleased, Juliette expressed how affectionately she had taken care of her hair. Prince quickly grew sick of the discussion and decided to participate in a talk with Rose. To amaze the young prince Geoffrey, Rose began to describe the court of her father and to talk about all the well-known personalities in it. After Prince Geoffrey was no longer able to hear he planned to see Isabella. He was awestruck by her prettiness as soon as he saw her. In Isabelle, Juliette and Rose scoffed, berating her messy hair. When the prince said she had pretty eyes, both Rose and Juliet clarified that all the sisters had pretty eyes. Geoffrey Prince told, "She is indeed blessed with gorgeous eyes. Still she's playing with toys! "Juliette answered, struggling to make Isabella look childish. "What, then? And I like to play with dolls. "Pulling a tiny doll out of his bag, he showed it to everybody as his bests friend, Jane. Delighted, Isabella introduced him to her new friends. She followed him to the garden when he agreed, leaving her mean sisters behind.

2.8. The Boy Who Cried Wolf

A carefree boy had been living with his father in a village. The father of the boy told him he was old enough to look after the sheep while they are grazing in the fields. He had to send herds of sheep to the grassy fields every day to see them graze. The boy was unhappy, however, and didn't want to take his sheep to the fields. He wanted to escape and play in the field, not look the boring sheep graze. So, he set out to have fun. He yelled, "Wolf! Wolf, wolf! "Till the whole village came running with stones to chase the wolf away, before any of the sheep could eat. When the villagers noticed that no wolf was there, they left to murmur under their breath about how their time had been wasted. The next day, the boy again shouted, "Wolf! Wolf, wolf! "And the villagers rushed to chase the wolf away, again.

The boy giggled at the scare he'd caused. The villagers left angrily this time. On third day, as the boy walked up the little hill, he saw a wolf suddenly attacked his sheep. He was screaming as much as he could," "Wolf! Wolf, wolf! Wolf, wolf! "But there came not a single villager to help him. The villagers assumed he was making them fool again, and didn't even come to rescue him and his sheep. That day the little boy lost many sheep, just because of his stupidity.

Moral of the Story

It is difficult to trust people who lie, so it's important to always be truthful.

2.9. The Fox and the Stork

One day, a stork invited a selfish fox to dinner. Stork was very pleased with the invitation-she came to the home of the fox on time and knocked with her long beak at the door. The fox took her to the dining room, and served some soup for both of them in shallow bowls. She couldn't have soup at all, as the dish was too small for the stork. But the fox quickly licked up his soup.

The stork was upset and angry, but she showed no anger, and behaved politically. She then called him to dinner the next day, to teach the fox a lesson. She also served soup but the soup was served in two tall narrow vases this time. The stork drank the soup from her vase, but due to his narrow neck the fox could not drink it at all. The fox realized his mistake, and went hungry at home.

Moral of the Story

Sooner or later a selfish act fire back!

2.10. The Golden Touch

A greedy man once lived in a small town. He was very wealthy, and he loved fantasy about gold and everything. But he more than anything had loved his dad. One day, he chanced upon a fairy. The fairy 's hair was trapped in a some tree branches. He helped her, but when his greed and selfishness took hold, he realized that he had a chance to become wealthier by asking for a reward in return (for helping her out). The fairy gave him a wish.

He said, "Everything that I touch should turn into gold." And the grateful fairy granted him his wish.

The greedy man ran home to tell his wife and daughter about his wish, all of the sudden touching and watching stones and pebbles convert into gold. His daughter rushed to salute him once he got home. She turned into a golden statue once he bent down to scoop her up in his arms. He was devastated, and began to cry and try to revive his daughter. He realized his foolishness and spent the rest of his days looking for the fairy to carry away his wishes.

Moral of the Story

Greed always contributes to destruction.

2.11. The Milk maid and Her Pail

A milkmaid named Patty was milking her cow and had two buckets full of creamy, fresh milk. She placed those two buckets of milk on a rod and went out to sell the milk in the market. As she moved to the market, her point of view turned towards wealth. She kept on wondering about the money that she was going to gain by selling the milk. Then she pondered what she was going to do with that income.

She was speaking to herself and she said, "I'll buy a chicken after I obtain the money. The chicks will lay eggs and I'll get too many chickens. They're all going to lay eggs and I'm going to sell the eggs for more profit. Today, I'm going to purchase the house on top of the hill and everybody's going to jealous of me. "She was so excited because she'd be very wealthy soon. She marched forward with those happy thoughts. But, eventually, she fell and tripped. Both the milk pails had fallen, and all her daydreams had been shattered. Milk spread on the ground and all the Patty would do is crying. "No more vision," she screamed dumbly!

Moral of the Story

Don't count your chicks before hatching.

2.12. When Adversity Knocks

This is a short story which illustrates how various individuals face challenges differently. A girl called Alice had been living in a village with her father and mother. One fine day, her dad assigned an easy task to her. He had taken three vessels full of boiling water. He put one egg in a container, the potato in the second one, and a few leaves of tea in the third. He advised Alice to keep a close eye on the containers for about 10-15 minutes, as the 3 ingredients boiled in three different containers. He asked Alice to peel the egg and the potato after the said time, and to strain the leaves of tea. Alice was left confused-she knew that she was attempting to clarify something to her father, but she didn't recognize what it was.

Her father clarified, "all three things were placed in the similar situations. See if they reacted differently. "He explained the potato became delicate, the egg became tough and tea leaves altered the water's color and taste. He said further, "We're all similar to one of those things. We react just the way they do when adversity calls. So, are you an egg, a potato, or tea leaves?"

Moral of the Story

We can decide how to react according to a situation.

2.13. The Proudy Rose

A lovely rose plant once stood in a greenhouse. One rose flora was very proud of its prettiness on the plant. Though, it was frustrated, that it grew alongside a dirty cactus. The rose would criticize the cactus for its appearance each day, whereas the cactus remained silent. All the other plant species in the yard advised to restrict the rose from harassing the cactus, however the rose was so influenced to listen to anybody because of its own beauty. One summer, there was no water as the well in the ground dried up.

The rose gradually began to wane. For some water, the rose looked the sparrow dip his beak in the cactus. The rose finally felt ashamed all this time for making fun of the cactus. But since it needed water, it left and asked cactus if it might have some water. A kindest cactus granted and both of them became friends.

Moral of the Story

Do not judge anyone by their looks.

2.14. The Tale of a Pencil

A boy called Stephen was angry regarding his English exam as he had performed terribly. His grandma came to him he was alone in his bed and supported him. His grandma sat next to him, and offered him a pencil. Stephen looked confused at his grandmother, and said despite his test results, he did not deserve a pencil.

His grandma clarified, "This pencil will tell you many things, because it's just like you. It feels an aching sharpening as the way you've felt the stress of not passing the exam well. It will however help you to become a good student. Just like all the success of the pencil comes from inside, you must also need the power to pass this obstacle. And eventually, just like this pencil is going to leave its mark on anything, you too are going to leave your mark on whatever you pick. "Stephen was instantly consoled and pledged to do better.

Moral of the Story

We've the power to become who we want to be.

2.15. The Crystal Ball

John, a little boy, found a ball of crystal behind his garden. The tree told him; it will award him a wish. He became very glad and thought a lot but he couldn't come up with something he wanted, sadly. So, he put the ball of crystal in his bag, waiting unless he could make a decision on his wish.

Days passed without making a wishing, but his friend caught him gazing at the ball of crystal. He took it from John, and then exposed it in the village for everyone. Many of them requested for palaces and prosperity and a lot of money, but couldn't create more than a wish. All was upset at the end that no one could get everything they needed. They got very upset, and planned to seek help from John. John wanted everything to go back to the way it once was – before the villagers attempted to fulfill their greed. All the gold and palaces disappeared, and the villagers became pleased and relaxed once again.

Moral of the Story

Wealth and money don't always lead to happiness.

2.16. Bundle of wooden Sticks

Once there were three neighbors were having difficulty with crops while living in a village. Each one of the neighbors had one meadow, but pests infested the harvests on their meadows, and they wilted. They would present innovative ideas every day to aid their crops. The former tried to use a scarecrow in his meadow, the latter used insecticides, and third make a wooden fence around his field.

One day the head of the village came over and called all the farmers. He provided each one a stick and ordered them to break it down. They could easily be broken by the farmers. He then offered them a 3-stick set, and again told them to split it. The farmers this time failed to break the bundle of sticks. The head of the village replied, "You are powerful together and work well than you can do it alone." All the farmers knew what the head of the village had been saying. They invested in their means and cleared their fields from the pests.

Moral of the Story

Unity is strength.

2.17. The Ant and the Dove

An ant was moving around in the search of water on a hot, scorching summer day. She saw a river after searching around for a while, and was happy to found it. She moves up up to drink the water on a tiny rock, but slipped down and fell down in the river. She was sinking but she was helped by a dove sitting on a neighboring tree. Finding the ant in danger, the dove dropped a leaf in the water quickly. The ant moved to the leaf, climbing onto it. The dove then took the leaf out carefully, and laid it on the ground. Thus, the life of the ant was protected, and she was deeply in debt to the dove forever.

The ant and the dove thus became best friends, and happily passed the days. One day, however, a hunter entered the forest. He had seen a lovely dove resting on the tree, and targeted at the dove with his weapon. The ant, that the dove rescued, saw it and little on the hunter's foot. He shouted out of ache and dropped his weapon. The hunter's voice alarmed the dove, and realized what might have happened to him. He actually fluttered away!

Moral of the Story

A good deed never goes unrewarded.

2.18. The Fox and the Grapes

A fox went through the jungle on a hot summer day to get something to eat. He looked for food very greedy and desperately. He looked all over, but could not find anything he was able to eat. He rumbled his stomach, and continued his quest. Shortly he came to a vineyard filled with ripe grapes. The fox began to look around to see if the hunters were safe. There was nobody there, so he wanted to pick a few grapes. He jumped up and up, but couldn't access the grapes. The grapes were so high but he did not give up. The fox hopped into the air and caught the grapes, but he did not. Again, he attempted, but again he failed. A couple more times he tried, but was not able to reach. It became dark and the fox became furious. He injured his legs and eventually gave up. He said, "anyways I'm sure that the grapes are sour," he walked forward.

Moral of the Story

An act of kindness never goes without reward.

2.19. The Ant and the Grasshopper

Two good friends once were there-an ant and a grasshopper. Grasshopper enjoyed relaxing and playing his guitar all day. The ant will work hard whole day though. He would gather food from every corner of the yard, whereas the grasshopper would relax, play his guitar, and sleep. The grasshopper would say daily to ant to have a break, but the ant might deny and carry on his work. Soon, winters came; cold days and nights and few insects came out.

A group of ants was too busy in drying out a few grains of corns on a cold winter day. Cold and hungry, the half-dead grasshopper went to the ant that was his companion and requested for a bit of corn. The ant answered, "We're working day and night to gather and save the corn thus we don't have to die of hungry during cold winter times. Why are we going to send you this? "The ant asked on," What did you do last summer? You must have gotten some food and stored it. I have told you the same before.

"I was just too busy sleeping and singing," the grasshopper said.

The ant responded, "As long as I am worried you can sing all winter. You won't get everything from us. "An ant had sufficient food to pass the winters without any troubles, but that didn't happen to the grasshopper and he admitted his fault.

Moral of the Story

Create hay during the sun shines.

2.20. The Bear and the Two Friends

One fine day, two friends walked through a jungle on a barren and risky road. As the sun arose, they became frightened but stayed close to each other. They suddenly looked a bear standing on their way. One of the guys ran and climbed the adjacent tree in a jiffy. The other guy himself didn't know how to climb up the tree, so he lay down on the floor, pretended to be dead. The big bear in the jungle approached the child, and smelled near his ears. The bear went on its way after it appeared to murmur something in the boy's ear. The boy climbed down on the tree and inquired from his companion what did the bear say in his ear. His friend responded, "Don't believe on friends who don't care about you."

Moral of the Story

A friend in need is a friend indeed.

2.21. Friends Forever

There once existed a frog and a mouse, who had become the best friends. The frog would jump out of the pond every morning to meet the mouse, who used to live inside the tree hole. He was going to enjoy time with a mouse, then go home. The frog realized one day that he made too much exertion to meet the mouse whereas the mouse hasn't ever come to visit him at the side of the pond. That made him mad and he thought to take him forcefully to his home to make things right.

The frog attached a rope to the tail of the mouse while the mouse was not watching, then knotted the other edge of his own leg, and then hopped backwards. The mouse got dragged along with him. The frog then hopped into the pond for swimming. When he turned up, though, he noticed the mouse had begun to drown and having difficulty in breathing! The frog rapidly unbound the cord from end of his tail, taking him down to the shore. Watching the mouse with barely open his eyes got the frog really sad and he quickly regretted dragging him into the water.

Moral of the Story

Do not take revenge, as it can do harm to you.

2.22. An Elephant and Her Friends

A lonely elephant once made its path into a weird jungle. It was different for her, and she'd been searching for companions. She approached a monkey and said, "Hi, ape! Would you accept to be my friend? "You're too heavy to swing like I do, the monkey said, so I can't be your mate." Then the elephant meets a rabbit and requested the same thing. "You're too large to live in my hole, so I can't be your mate," the rabbit said. The elephant then went to the pond frog and repeated the same query. "You're too big to climb as high as i, so I can't be your mate" answered the frog.

The elephant was truly lonely, as she was unable to make friends. And, one fine day, she noticed all the wildlife running further into the woods and inquired a bear about what the trouble was. The bear answered, "The lion is coming and they are going to secure themselves." Elephant reached to the lion and requested, "Please don't harm these poor people. Leave them please. "The lion laughed and ordered the elephant to go away. The elephant then got furious and moved the lion with all her strength, wounding him. All of the other animals slowly came out, and began to rejoice over the defeat of the lion. They came to the elephant and told her that You are the perfect size for being our friend!"

Moral of the Story

The size of a person doesn't determine his or her worth.

2.23. The Woodcutter and the Golden Axe

Once upon a time there was a woodcutter, doing very work hard in the forest, cutting wood to sale for food. Accidentally his axe dropped into the river as he was cutting a tree. The river was too deep and very fast flowing. He misplaced his axe and couldn't find it. He stood on the river shore, and cried.

While he was weeping, the river Angel appeared and inquired from him what had happened. The woodcutter explained the story to him. The river Angel agreed to help him finding his axe. He vanished in the river and found a golden axis, but then the woodcutter told it wasn't his. He vanished again and returned with a silver axis, but the woodcutter said that it wasn't his either. The Angel disappeared again in the water and returned with an axe made of iron. The woodcutter nodded and told it was his axe. The Angel was pleased by the sincerity of the woodcutter, and gave him the silver and golden axes.

Moral of the Story

Honesty is the best policy.

2.24. Princess and the Triangle of Sorcery

On one glorious day in the palace yard, the princess of the Norfolk Kingdom discovered a ring. When she asked her dad about the ring, he informed him that five special powers would bring her:

- Ability to sleep quietly.
- Working without a flint.
- The freedom to grow the plant of its choosing.
- The opportunity to rain without any sky clouds.
- Ability, like an enchanted siren, to sing.

The fifth was the most popular power of the princess. She would sing for long, hoping one day for her lovely voice a charming prince would fall.

The Empire became stupid one day with a trick of a witch. All but the princess was affected. The witch took away all that it had, including the sun, fire, rains and plants, from the kingdom. The princess was devastated by the wretched condition of her country. But her five extraordinary forces were all she had to support her country! Her mind came up with a spontaneous idea: she hurried to the balcony and began to sing. For months, the princess sang all night and day. When her parents asked her, she won't discourage. The kingdom became stabilized after a year or two of singing. Yet the princess vanished in the storm at the same moment. Because of the sacrifices of the princess, the reign restored to its original glory.

2.25. The Princess & the Pea

Once upon a time there lived a prince looking for a good princess. He was looking for the right one across seven oceans, but he wasn't confident if the princesses he found were real. He finally returned home, disheartened.

A devastating thunderstorm occurred one evening. The queen opened the door after hearing a knock at the door. In muddy and soiled clothes there was a princess. Her hair seemed ugly; her shoes had been thoroughly drenched with mud. She claimed she was a genuine princess. "We must discover the facts early," the queen said. The queen came to the bedroom and pulled all the mattresses from the bed. Then she put a pea on the bottom and placed twenty mattresses over it. Next she set up the mattresses of twenty feathered beds. For that night the princess had to sleep on the bed. The queen asked the princess in the morning about her sleep quality. "I really couldn't able to sleep all night," the princess replied. The queen then realized that, indeed, she was a true princess, as only a genuine princess would feel the pain through the feathered beds and twenty mattresses. The prince chooses her as his wife, recognizing that she was a genuine queen.

2.26. The Princess and the Faithful Knight

There was once a princess, whose elegance was not only to talk about her own region but to talk about in a lot of a country. The princess was brought up to be fair and honest, as pretty as she was. As the days passed her only worry was the enjoyment and pleasure of her people. One good day a prince came to the kingdom for the princess' trial. Both stayed together for hours, days and weeks. The princess fell in love with the lovely prince.

Another day the prince brought his princess to creepy grassland filled with flowers, near the forest's edge. He confronted the princess, who really loved him, to pick his rare flower — the scarlet went up from the thick forests. The princess went into the forest to look for the rose scarlet. She liked the prince, so she was going to show that to him. She saw a lovely flower when she just gave up. The princess fascinated with her beauty and touched her, but fell asleep immediately.

The prince appeared suddenly. He decided to steal the princess' wealth and jewelry. He took the precious things and forsook the princess. The king sent his soldiers wide and far to look after her, when the princess did not come back to her father. They found her in the meadow, covered by vine, after a long search.

His consultants found she had touched a rose scarlet and therefore could not be awakened. The King attempted to pick her up with every step and drink, but nothing improved.

The disappointed king revealed that whoever could wait on the side of the princesses before she woke would get her hand for marriage. Many of the followers were drawn by the beauty of the princesses, but she was not aware of her sleep. Her beauty faded as time went by, just as many of the followers did, except one-man, who knelt and had not been moving since the time of his arrival. When the princess got up, she found her faithful knight standing next to her. He informed her of the poison and order of the King and claimed her unending devotion. The King was glad that his daughter had returned, and that she got a loving husband and then the next day king announced their wedding.

2.27. Princess Rose and the Golden Bird

A lovely princess who had stunning red hair and cherished roses existed in a distant land a long time ago. Princess Rose was her name. Princess Rose will also come out and clap her hands every night on her balcony. A little golden bird will emerge and land on her shoulder when she saw her. The hair of the princesses will have a lovely red luster, and she with the bird will sing a love song, which would let everyone to sleep.

One fine day, Princess Rose was spelled by a jealous witch and turned her pretty red hair to black. The kingdom had hallucinations and unpleasant dreams that night when the princess and the bird sang. The bird asked the princess to rinse the hair in pink rose water, and everything would be fine again. The princess rinsed her hair with pink rose water, and kingdom people fell asleep.

When the wicked witch heard it, Princess Rose turned her hair black; this time, then all the roses disappeared in the country. The princess emerged with a ray of red hair as Princess Rose screamed out in sorrow. The lovely red rose, as her eyes reached her hair and Princess Rose again may dye her hair red. The Prince disclosed that as a sign of loyalty he and the princess had swapped a hair strand as children.

The prince and Rose were married and lived together after all, and the wicked witch got so furious that she burst into a million pieces.

2.28. The Needle Tree

Two brothers lived close to a forest. For the younger brother the older one was tremendous mean — he'd eat all of the food and dress his younger brother's new clothing. One fine day, the oldest brother planned to get firewood from the forest and sell that in the market . He stumbled upon a magical tree while he went all around, chopping tree by tree. "Oh mister, don't cuts my branches, please, the tree requested. If you spare me, I'll reward you golden apples, he accepted, but was dissatisfied by the amount of apples that the tree offered him. When he was overcome by covetousness, he threatened that the tree would cut the whole trunk unless it gave him more apples. On the contrary, the magical tree showered hundreds of tiny needles over the elder brother. The older brother was sitting on the floor, crying with distress as the sun was setting.

He got concerned about the younger brother, so he went to seek his elder brother. His body was hundreds of needles and he found him lie in pain near the tree. His brother rushed and lovingly and softly removed all needles. When he was done, the older brother excused him and pledged to be better. He won't treat him negatively. The tree had seen the transformation in the heart of the elder brother and gave them all the apples they ever needed.

Moral of the story

It is essential, as it will still be rewarded, to be kind and gracious.

2.29. The Greedy Lion

A lion in the forest had started to feel hungry on a hot day. When he saw a hare wandering alone around, he began searching for his meal. Instead of capturing the hare, the lion let it go – he said and scoffed, "A little hare like this can't fulfill my appetite" Then a pretty deer went by and he wanted to take his chances – he fled and chased behind the deer, but he tried to keep up with the pace of the deer because he was poor because of the hunger. Tired and defeated, for the time being the lion went back to look for the hare to fill his stomach but it was gone. The lion was lonely, and was long starving.

Moral of the story

Greed is never healthy.

2.30. The Lion & The Poor Slave

A slave runs away to the jungle, untreated by his owner. He finds a lion in pain because of his paw's thorn. The slave goes forward bravely and gently removes the thorn.

The lion goes away, without hurting.

A couple of days later, the owner of the slave comes to the forest to kill other livestock and cages. The masters' people see the slave capturing him and taking him to the ruthless master.

The owner demands that the slave be put into the enclosure of the lion.

When the slave was waiting in the cage for death, he realizes that he is the same lion that he helped he is w. The lion and all the other animals in cages were rescued the slave.

Moral of the story:

One must help others in need, in exchange for the benefits of our helpful actions.

2.31. An Old Man in the Village

An elderly man used to live in a village. He was the world's poorest man. The entire village got sick of him; as he was constantly dull, he complained the misfortune constantly became infectious. Even being happy according to him was abnormal and disrespectful always seemed to be in bad mood.

In others, he made people feel unhappy.

And one day, at the age of eighty, something unbelievable happened. All of them began to hear the rumor immediately:

He doesn't criticize whatsoever, smiles and his face is renewed. "An Old Man's happy today.

The entire village was gathered. He told the old man.

Villager: What is the reason?

"Nothing is special. I've chased joy for 80 years, and it has been pointless. And instead I chose to live without pleasure and only enjoy life. And now I'm happy.

Moral of the story:

Don't follow happiness. Appreciate your life.

2.32. A Wise Man

People have come to a wise man, each time they complain about the similar problems. One fine day he was asking everyone a story and everybody was laughing with laughter.

He told them the very same joke after a few minutes and only two of them laughed.

No-one smiled as he told the same story for the third time.

Smiled the wise man, and said:

"You can't carry on smiling at the same story. So why do you always cry over the same issue?"

Moral of the story:

Worrying isn't going to fix the problems, it'll just drain the energy and time.

2.33. The Foolish Donkey

Every day a salt vendor took the salt bag to the market on his donkey.

They'd needed to pass a lake on the road. The donkey suddenly fell down the stream one day and the salt bag fell into the water too. The salt was dissolved in the water and this made the bag very lightweight to carry. The donkey was overjoyed.

The donkey then started playing the same tactic daily. The salt seller has come to understand his trick, and has decided to teach it a lesson. He loaded a cotton bag onto the donkey the next day. Again he performed the same trick thinking the cotton bag would get lighter again. Yet it became really hard to bear the dampened fabric, and the donkey cried. It had taught a lesson. Since that day he no longer played the trick and the seller was satisfied.

Moral of the story:

Luck will not always favorable.

2.34. The Golden Egg

A farmer once had a pigeon which lay a gold egg daily. The egg supplied the farmer and his wife with enough money to satisfy their daily needs. For a long time, the farmer and his wife were pleased. When one day the farmer had an idea and he said to himself, "Why would I only take one egg per day? Why can't I take them all in one go and produce a lot of revenue?

Also the foolish farmer's wife accepted and wanted to cut the eggs from the pigeon's stomach. Once the bird was killed and the pigeon's stomach opened, they found nothing but intestinal tract and blood. Realizing his foolish fault, the farmer started crying over the lost asset!

Also from this classic tale was taken the English idiom "destroy not the pigeon which lays the gold egg."

Moral of the story

Think before you act.

2.35. The Miser And His Gold

An old miser had been living in a gardened house. In the field, the miser concealed his gold coins in a trap under some rocks. Every day, the miser see the rocks where he buried the gold and numbered the coins, before he goes to the bed. Each day he practiced this practice but he did not spend that gold he collected once.

One day, a robber who recognized the schedule of the old miser was waiting for the rich man to come home. The robber moved to the burying-place after it was darker and stole the gold. The day after, the old miser finds his treasure lacking, and started to weep loudly.

His neighbor heard the scream of the miser, and asked what had happened. The neighbor asked on learning, "Why didn't you bury the gold in your house?" Accessing the money would have been easier when you needed to buy anything!

"Buy?" the miser replied. "I used nothing of the gold to purchase anything. I will never use it.'

Upon learning this, the neighbor dropped a stone into the hole and replied, "Save the stone, if this is the case. It's as useless as you've missed the money.

Moral of the story

A property is equally deserving of what it is being used to.

2.36. The Tortoise And The Bird

Under a tree rested a tortoise, on which a bird had established its nest. The tortoise mockingly asked the creature, "What a messy house you have! It's made of cracked twigs and it doesn't have a roof and looks simple. What worse is, you've had to construct this yourself. I believe my home is much perfect than your pitiful nest, that is my "shell".

"Yes it's constructed of broken rocks, it looks dirty and it's vulnerable to nature's elements. It's rough, but I made it, so I like it.'

"I think it is like every other nest, but its not stronger than mine," the tortoise said. "But you've got to be jealous of my cover."

"On the other hand" replied the bird. "My house has room for my friends and family; your shell can't fit anyone else except you. You may have a better house in there. Now I've got a great house,' the bird said happily.

Moral of the story

Better a crowded hut than a lonely mansion.

2.37. The Cows And The Tiger

Four cows had lived near a grassy field in a forest. They have been good buddies and they have done everything with each other. They grazed and lived together so no tigers or lions will attack them for food.

Yet one day the friends clashed and every cow went in a separate direction to graze. A tiger and a lion noticed that, and thought it was the best opportunity to slaughter the animals. They hid themselves in the woods and shocked the horses, killing all of them, one by one.

Moral of the story

Unity is strength.

2.38. The Four Students

Four classmates had disliked school. They took part the night before their tests and decided to fail the study by lying to the teacher. So they ended up going to the headmaster and told him the last night they had been to a wedding and they had a broken car on the way back. They proceeded to claim they needed to drive the vehicle all the way back, because they had no extra tire yet were were not in a condition to submit the test. The dean paid attention and approved on taking the test on later day. they got Happy to get a second opportunity, the four friends have been studying hard and ready for the exam. On the day before the exam the dean told the students to remain in different classes, which was accepted by the students.

There were just two questions in the exam board, for a minimum of 100 points. The questions, then, were:

- Your name:

- Which vehicle tire burst:

a) Front right

b) Front left

c) Rear right

d) Rear left

Moral of the story

You might be wise, but the universe has people that are wiser than you.

2.39. The Boasting Traveler (Aesop's Fables)

A man from a tour returned and bragged about his adventurous tours. He spoke at length about various people he knows and his wonderful feats that gave him everywhere fame and appreciate from people. He went on to explain that he came to the Rhodes where he may have sprung so far that no one could ever fit his feat.

He even continued to say there were eyewitness who were going to attest for his words. A smart bystander, listening the man brag so much, said, "Oh good man, we don't require any witnesses to consider your words. Imagine Rhodes being this position and running towards us.

The dishonest traveler did not know what to do or how and quietly walked away.

Moral of the story

One who does a good thing shouldn't claim.

2.40. The Camel And The Baby

One fine day, a camel and her baby were talking to each other. The kid said, "Mother, why do we even have humps?" the mother answered, "Our humps are built to hold water so we can live in the deserts."

"Oh," the child stated, "and why we have curved feet mum?"
"Because they are supposed to help us travel safely in the desert. These limbs help us walk in the sand."

"Exactly. But why we have long eyelashes?" To save our eyes from the sand and dust of the desert. For the eyes, they are the preventive covers, "the mother camel replied.

For quite a while, the baby camel figured and said, "We have humps to store water for trips through the desert, curved hooves to make us relaxed walking in the desert sand, and have long eyelashes to save us from dust and sand in a desert storm. So, What will we do in a zoo?

The mum was stupid.

Moral of the story

If you're not in the right place, your strengths, your skills and your knowledge are useless.

2.41. The Farmer And The Well

A farmer searching for a water supply for his farm has purchased a well from his friend. However, the friend was cunning and refused to allow the farmer to take the water out of the well. He replied, "I offered you the well, but not water," wondering why, and walking away. The distressed farmer had no clued what to do. So, he went for an answer to Birbal, a wise guy and one of Emperor Akbar's nine courtiers.

The king called the farmer and his friend and inquired why the man wouldn't let the farmer take water out of the well. Again the clever man said same thing, "I sold the well but not water. He can't take my water, therefore.

Birbal responded, "To me it all sounds just fine. But if you've sold the well and the water is all yours, then you don't have to keep your water in its well. Remove water, or instantly consume it all up. If you do not, the water belongs to the well's owner.'

On realizing he's been fooled and his lesson taught, the guy apologized and left. **Moral of the story**

Cheating doesn't offer everything to you. If you ever lie, you will soon be paying for it.

3.42. The Wolf And The Shepherds

This is one of several fables in Aesop to which one can relate in anyday age.

A wolf ran away from the farm one day for attempting to steal any of the sheep for food. The wolf returned to the farm later that week, desperate to find some food. He peeped within the house, and found a lamb roast feast for the farmer and his family.

"Ah! "He assumed "If I would be doing the same stuff the farmer and his family are now doing, I would be shunned and persecuted, or even murdered for killing a feeble, victimized lamb."

Moral of the story

We're fast to judge and criticize others for what they're doing, but see nothing bad with our own doing so.

3.43. The Young Crab And His Mother

One day, there was a young crab on the beach with his mum, spending time with each other. The young crab is going to go up but it can still move sideways. His mom scolded him for stepping sideways and asked him to go forward, attempting to point his toes out from the front. The young crab replies, "I want to move forward mother, but I don't know how to do it."

On listening this, his mother gets up to teach him how, but she can not even bend her knees over. She admits she was wrong, apologies herself sheepishly and sits down in the sand.

Moral of the story

Don't blame others for failing to achieve what you can not manage yourself.

3.44. The Other Side Of The Wall

A young woman had inherited her grandmother's beautiful garden. She also loved gardening, and was extremely proud of her orchard. One day she saw in a catalog a really beautiful plant and she wanted it for her orchard. She bought it, and planted it in her backyard at the base of the stonewall. She took special care of the plant which developed rapidly and had lovely green leaves on it.

Months elapsed but there was not even a single flower blooming on the rose. Vexed, she had almost needed to reduce down the tree. Her invalid called at such a time, and said, "Thank you very much for the pretty flowers. You don't know how much I love seeing the vine blooms you've planted.

On listening this, the young girl runs to the side of a wall of the neighbor and sees in flower the most exquisite flora. All the care that she had done had paid off. Just the vine seeped through the crevices, due to which it didn't bloom on the side of the wall, but on the other side it did generously.

Moral of the story

Only because you can't see the good outcomes of your efforts doesn't mean it doesn't yield results.

3.44. The Star Money

Once, there was a small girl whose dad and mom were dead. She was really poor she had no more tiny space to live in, or room to sleep. Finally, she had little more but the clothing she was carrying and a small piece of bread in her hand which she had been given by some generous person. And she was decent and pious.

And as the entire world had thus forsaken her, she went out into the open land, believing in the good God.

A poor man then met her, saying, "Ah, bring me anything to feed, I'm starving"

She reached only those her slice of bread to him, and told, "May God bless it for your use," and moved on.

Then a child came up moaning and told, "My head has become so cold, offer me anything to cover it."

So she removed her hat, and offered it to him.

And since she had traveled just a little further she found another girl who had no sweater and was cold-frozen. She then handed it her own.

She asked for a frock a little more for that, so she gave away one too.

She finally came into woods and it had already turned dark, and another child came up and inquired for just a little shirt. The decent little girl thought to herself, "It's a dark at night and nobody's looking at me. I can give away my little shirt really well, "stripped it off, and threw it away, too.

So she stayed that way, because there was not an option left. Then some heavenly Stars suddenly fell down, and they had been nothing but hard, seamless parts of money. And even if she'd just given away her little shirt, lo! She had quite a new one, of the finest linen. She then collected the money into that, and every day of her life she became happy.

3.45. Jorinda and Joringel

Once upon a time there was an old castle in the center of a wide and dense wood, and all alone dwelt in it an old lady, who was a wicked Witch.

She transformed herself to a cat in the daylight, but she took her proper form again in the evening as a human being . She might attract her wild beasts and animals, so she would destroy and cook and bake them.

If anybody came in the hundred places of the castle, he was forced to stand still and was unable to move from the place till she blesses him to get free. But if a poor maiden came into this circle, she transformed her into a pigeon, locked her up in a carved wooden-work cage, and took the cage to the castle room. In the castle she had around seven thousand bird cages of rare birds.

Now, once there was a maiden named Jorinda, who was fair and equitable than any other girl. She and a beautiful boy named Joringel had decided to marry each other, and being together was their greatest happiness.

One day, they went for a walk in the forest in order to be able to talk together in silence. "Watch out," Joringel said, "that you don't go too close to the castle."

It was a splendid evening. The sun was shining brightly between both the trees 'trunks into the forest's dark green, and the turtledoves started singing sorrowfully upon the birch-trees' young boughs.

Jorinda was weeping here and there. She stood in the sunlight, and felt miserable. Joringel too was sad. They were as depressed as if on the verge of death. So they looked about and were struggling quite a bit, so they didn't know how to get there. Half above the mountain was the sky, and half mounted.

Joringel looked across the woods, and saw the castle 's old walls close by. He was hit with terror and packed with mortal fear.

Jorinda was singing:

"My tiny bird, with a red necklace, sings sorrow, sorrow, sorrow, he sings, the dove must be dead soon, he sings sorrow, sorrow, sorr---jug, jug, jug"

Joringel searched out for Jorinda. She became a Nightingale, and sang "jug, jug, jug"

A screech-owl with glittering eyes soared over her three times and screamed three times, "to-whoo, to-whoo, to-whoo, to-whoo, to-whoo"

Joringel was not able to move about. He did stand like a stone there, and could neither cry nor talk, nor move his hand or his foot.

Now, the sun had set. The owl walked through the thicket. A crooked old lady, yellow and slim, with wide red eyes and a twisted nose, the tip of which touched her lip, emerged out of it immediately afterwards. She mumbled to herself, grabbed the Nightingale, and took him away into her hand.

Joringel was unable to speak or to move from its spot. The Nightingale died.

Finally the woman returned, and said in a flat voice, "Greet thee, Zachiel. Zachiel, let him loose at once if the moon shines on the cage.'

Then they released Joringel. He dropped to the woman's knees and pleaded that she should restore his Jorinda to him. But she insisted he would never ever have her, and instead left. He called, weeping. He argued, but everything was in vain, "Ah, what's to become of me"

Joringel was gone, and came to a different village at last. He kept herds there for a longer period. He frequently walked around the castle but not so close to it. One night he dreamed that he discovered a Blood-Red Flower, in the center of which was a magnificent big pearl; that he picked up the flower and went to the castle with it, and that all he reached with the flower was set free from transformation. He also dreamed of having his Jorinda recovered through it.

When he awoke in the morning, he began looking over the hill and dale to find such flower. He tried the Blood-Red Flower till the ninth day, and then, soon in the morning, discovered it.

There was a big dew-drop in the middle of it, as large as the best pearl.

He 'd traveled to the castle with this flower day and night. He did not hold fast while he was and within hundred laps of it, but started walking towards the door.

Joringel was brimming with joy. With the flower he reached the screen, and it sprung open. He moved through the courtyard, listening to the birds' music. He had finally heard it. He moved on, and discovered the room where it came from. There the wicked Witch was in the seven thousand cages feeding the birds.

She was mad, very mad, and scolded spat the poison and gall when she saw Joringel, but within two paces of him she couldn't even come. He took no care of her but went with the birds and stared at the cages. But there were hundreds of Nightingales, how could he locate his Jorinda again?

Merely then he saw the old white woman quietly pulling a cage with a pigeon in it, and going up to the door.

He jumped for her instantly, reached the cage along with the flower, and the old lady too.

She couldn't bewitch someone anymore. And Jorinda stood there, clasping him around his arm, and she was as radiant as ever!

CPSIA information can be obtained
at www.ICGtesting.com
Printed in the USA
BVHW041405100221
599801BV00005B/104